1 (510) 936-3000

THE POWER
OF YOUR POTENTIAL

Hey Sarah I ALSO wanted to send a note to some of my christian friends of some things I've learned if you might want to help it out it could be helpful

Books by Dr. John C. Maxwell
Can Teach You How to Be a REAL Success

Relationships

25 Ways to Win with People
Becoming a Person of Influence
Encouragement Changes Everything
Ethics 101
Everyone Communicates, Few Connect
The Power of Partnership
Relationships 101
Winning with People

Equipping

The 15 Invaluable Laws of Growth
The 17 Essential Qualities of a Team Player
The 17 Indisputable Laws of Teamwork
Developing the Leaders Around You
How Successful People Grow
Equipping 101
JumpStart Your Growth
JumpStart Your Priorities
Learning from the Giants
Make Today Count
Mentoring 101
My Dream Map
Partners in Prayer
Put Your Dream to the Test
Running with the Giants
Talent Is Never Enough
Today Matters
Wisdom from Women in the Bible
Your Road Map for Success

Attitude

Attitude 101
The Difference Maker
Failing Forward
Intentional Living
The Greatest Story Ever Told (journal)
How Successful People Think
JumpStart Your Thinking
The Power of Significance
Sometimes You Win—Sometimes You Learn
Sometimes You Win—Sometimes You Learn for Teens
Success 101
Thinking for a Change
The Winning Attitude

Leadership

The 5 Levels of Leadership
The 21 Indispensable Qualities of a Leader
The 21 Irrefutable Laws of Leadership, 10th Anniversary Edition
The 21 Most Powerful Minutes in a Leader's Day
The 360-Degree Leader
Developing the Leader within You
JumpStart Your Leadership
Good Leaders Ask Great Questions
Go for Gold
How Successful People Lead
Leadership 101
Leadership Gold
Leadership Promises for Every Day
The Power of Your Leadership
What Successful People Know about Leadership

THE POWER
OF YOUR POTENTIAL

HOW TO BREAK THROUGH
YOUR LIMITS

JOHN C. MAXWELL

CENTER
STREET

NEW YORK   NASHVILLE

The author is represented by Yates & Yates, LLP, Literary Agency, Orange, California.

Center Street
Hachette Book Group
1290 Avenue of the Americas, New York, NY 10104
centerstreet.com
twitter.com/centerstreet

Originally published as *No Limits* in hardcover and e-book in March 2017 by Center Street

First edition: May 2018

Center Street is a division of Hachette Book Group, Inc. The Center Street name and logo are trademarks of Hachette Book Group, Inc.

The publisher is not responsible for websites (or their content) that are not owned by the publisher.

The Hachette Speakers Bureau provides a wide range of authors for speaking events. To find out more, go to www.HachetteSpeakersBureau.com or call (866) 376-6591.

Library of Congress Control Number: 2017963559

ISBNs: 978-1-4555-4830-9 (hardcover), 978-1-4555-4831-6 (ebook)

Printed in the United States of America

LSC-C

10 9 8 7 6 5 4 3

To Kevin Myers

*I've observed you for more than thirty years, and
I've been part of your life for twenty. Your hunger to grow,
lead, and make a difference has set the tone for your life,
and I've watched you blow the cap off your capacity
time after time.*

*As much as anyone I know, you have proven that
people can overcome the limits put on them by themselves and
others. And your greatest impact is still ahead of you.*

Contents

PART II—CHOICES: DO THE THINGS THAT MAXIMIZE YOUR POTENTIAL

Acknowledgments

Thank you to:

Charlie Wetzel, my writer

Stephanie Wetzel, my initial manuscript editor

Linda Eggers, my executive assistant

INTRODUCTION

Are You Aware of Your Full Potential?

If you're like most people, I bet you'd like more out of life than you are currently experiencing. Maybe you're not succeeding in all the ways you desire to in life. Perhaps you're less than fully satisfied with your progress. Are you getting done all that you want to do? Or do you want to see more, do more, be more?

What's getting in your way? What's limiting you? Do you know? If you don't know what's limiting you, how will you remove it?

You've probably heard the saying "If I always do what I've always done, I'll always get what I've always gotten." I want to help you do something new—and get somewhere new. As we embark on this journey, I want to give you two thoughts:

1. Change doesn't always have to be drastic to be effective.
2. Change is necessary for you to reach your potential.

As you read through this book, be on the lookout for where you need to change your focus to become more aware of your potential. In part 1, on ability, you will be asked to work on some things that may not be natural strengths. You will find that difficult. Growth in skill areas, if they are not natural, is often slow and small. That's OK. Every little bit of positive change helps. However, when you get to part 2, which is about choices, you will find it to be easier. In matters of choice, changes can be achieved much more quickly. All of these changes, whether difficult or easy, need to be made if you desire to reach your full potential.

I want to help you expand your thinking and your ability. I want you to accept the challenge of releasing the power of your potential and changing your life. Are you willing to do that? If so, the process begins with awareness, with learning...

1. Your Potential Isn't Set

Have you given much thought to your potential? Most people think theirs is set. We hear one person identified as "high capacity" and another as "low capacity," and we just accept it. What's your capacity? Have you defined it as high, low, or average? Do you think it's set? Maybe you haven't put a label on it, but you've probably settled into a level of achievement that you believe is what's possible for you.

That's a problem.

Too many people hear the word *capacity* and assume it's a limitation. They assume their capacity is set—especially if they're beyond a certain age. People give up on the idea that their capacity or their potential can grow. All they do is try to manage whatever they think they've got. That's too confining. Instead, we need to define our world and ourselves in terms of our possibilities.

While I believe 100 percent that people can grow, change their capacity, and increase their potential, I also acknowledge that all of us have caps on our capacity. Some caps are fixed, but most are not. We can't allow these unfixed caps to keep our lives from expanding. We can't let caps define our potential. We need to look beyond the caps and see our true potential.

2. You Can Become Aware of the Possibilities That Can Make You Better

All lasting growth requires awareness. Unfortunately, if you lack awareness, then you don't know that you are unaware. It's a blind spot. You don't know what you don't know, and you can't see that you are unable to see. That's a catch-22.

Self-awareness is a powerful skill. It enables you to see yourself clearly. It informs your decisions and helps you to weigh opportunities. It allows you to test your limits. It empowers you to understand other people. It makes partnerships with others stronger. It allows you to maximize your strengths and minimize your weaknesses. It opens the door to greater potential.

Here are some things to think about as you work to become more aware of your possibilities:

ATTENTION: LOOKING FOR WHAT YOU NEED TO KNOW

We naturally tend to see things as we have always seen them. If we want to increase our potential, we must see differently. We need to be willing to look at ourselves and our world in new ways. We need to pay attention and look for what we need to know.

AWARENESS: DISCOVERING WHAT YOU NEED TO KNOW

What stops people from reaching their potential often isn't lack of desire but lack of awareness. Unfortunately, people don't become self-aware accidentally. On top of that, factors such as excuses, success fantasies that are ungrounded in reality, talking without listening to others, unresolved negative emotions, habitual self-distraction, absence of personal reflection, and unwillingness to pay the price to gain experience all work against us and prevent us from developing greater self-awareness.

Most people who have developed self-awareness have had to battle one or more of these factors to get where they are. They've had to work very hard. It takes desire to make self-awareness discoveries. It takes discipline to look at yourself and reflect on your experiences. It takes maturity to ask others to help you with your blind spots.

Becoming self-aware also requires help from other people who can see you more clearly than you can see yourself. You need to find someone—a trusted friend, colleague, mentor, or family member—who can help you, direct you, and provide you with repeated honest feedback.

DISCERNMENT: FOCUSING ON WHAT YOU NEED TO DO

As you discover things about yourself, you must try to discern where to focus your attention. You can't do everything, so focus on your strengths. When we focus on our weaknesses, the best we can do is work our way up to average. Nobody pays for that. No successful person hires someone to do a merely adequate job. Successful people desire excellence. Excellence comes from focusing on your strengths. Whatever you do well, try to do it better. That's your greatest pathway forward to increased potential.

INTENTION: ACTING ON WHAT YOU NEED TO DO

In my book *Intentional Living*, I discuss the major difference between good intentions and intentional living. The former may make a person feel good, but it doesn't actually do anything positive for that person or for others. The key is action. We get results only when we take what we've learned and put it into action.

You need to become aware that you are currently living below your potential if you're going to do anything to improve. Even if you've been a highly productive and successful person, you can improve. You can increase your potential. You have more in you that you have never tapped. And there is a path forward to greater potential if you are willing to take it.

3. You Can Remove the Caps from Your Capacity

The next step in increasing your potential involves removing the caps that are holding you back. We often believe that some of the restrictions we experienced earlier in life are permanent, or we've been told we have limitations that we actually don't possess, and these things keep us from taking the journey in life that we long for. These are the chains we need to break.

Awareness changes everything. As soon as we become

aware that some of our "limitations" are artificial, we can begin to overcome them. We can blow off these caps on our capacity, which opens the way for growth. I'll talk more about this later.

4. You Can Develop the Potential You Already Possess

Everyone has potential based on their natural talents. Some areas of potential require very specific abilities, such as those found in symphony musicians, professional athletes, and great artists. Other areas are more general in nature and rely on multiple skill sets. In part 1 of this book, I'll identify and examine seven of those areas, and I'll teach you how to maximize the talent you have so that you can increase your potential in each of these areas.

5. You Can Make Choices That Maximize Your Possibilities

You also have other areas of greater potential that rely more on your choices. While it's true that talent is still a factor, it is less important in these areas. I want to help you identify the choices you can make to increase your potential. In part 2, I'll teach you how to do that. And when you pair the development of your potential with the maximization of your choices, you start to develop personal momentum. Momentum is not the result of one push. It is the result of many continual pushes over time.

How Far Can You Go?

Maybe as you start this journey you should tell yourself that you're at only 40 percent of your potential. What would happen if you assumed that you had at least 60 percent more capacity than you ever believed? There's more in you that you've never tapped. What if it's not 60 percent? What if it's only 40, or 25, or even 10 percent? Wouldn't that still change your life? Believing there's more and working to tap into it could be a first step in reimagining your potential and embracing a no-limits life.

Caps You *Can't* Remove

I believe you can live a life with no limits, that you can go further than you believe and can do more than you've ever dreamed. But that doesn't mean that you don't possess limitations. We all do. Some caps cannot be removed.

Think about some of the caps in your life that you need to acknowledge and accept:

Birth caps: You had no control over where or when you were born, nor can you go back in time and change these things. You don't get to choose your parents, birth order, siblings, or upbringing. Good or bad, you have to live with these circumstances and make the best of them. You cannot change your genetic makeup, your race, your bone structure, or your height.

Life caps: There are many things that happen to us in our lives that we cannot control. We suffer accidents or illnesses. We lose people we love. We discover that we don't have the talent or ability to fulfill a dream. I call these "life caps." We all have life-cap stories, some big, some small. We have our nicks and dents. Part of the process of fulfilling your purpose is becoming aware of the things you can't change that limit you, so that you can direct your attention toward the things you *can* change to increase your capacity.

Caps You *Can* Remove

Too many people who aren't as successful, productive, and fulfilled as they would like to be mistakenly think they've worked through their issues, they've reached their capacity, and there are no new mountains they can climb. They settle. And they get comfortable.

Let me tell you: you're not even close to your potential. You haven't come close to reaching your limits. If you're willing to believe you have more potential and to work at making the most of it, you'll be amazed by the gains you can make. To get started, you need to remove the two main types of caps people have on their lives.

Caps That Others Put on Us

The first type of limitation comes from the caps that others put on us. People have put caps on you. You're not even aware of some of them. But you don't have to let others' lack of belief define you. Be unwilling to surrender your potential to someone else. Be unwilling to allow others to put caps on you and define your potential. You've fought too hard to get where you are to let others control where you are going. Be open to the possibilities that are in you!

Caps We Put on Ourselves

Perhaps the caps that limit us most are the ones we put on ourselves. But we don't have to leave them in place. We don't have to be limited by them forever. I think back to some of the caps I put on myself:

LOOKING FOR APPROVAL FROM OTHERS

When I started in my career, I was a people pleaser. I wanted to be everybody's favorite, and I didn't like rocking the boat. That's not a good mind-set if you want to be a leader. I had to learn how to remove that cap. I had to be willing to do what was right or what was best for the organization, even if it made people unhappy or I received criticism.

LIVING IN A LIMITING ENVIRONMENT

Too many people simply accept whatever environment they're born into. They think it's normal, and they start to believe they don't have any other choices in life. When that happens, they've created a self-imposed cap on their life. I grew up in a small town in a very conservative environment, where leadership wasn't valued or taught. I wanted to make a difference, and when I began to learn about leadership, I realized that I needed to move from that environment if I wanted to keep growing, learning, and expanding my potential.

HAVING FEW EXPANSIVE MODELS OF SUCCESS

When I was a senior in college and was getting ready to become a pastor, I wanted to someday lead a church of five hundred people. To me that was a bold goal, because a church of five hundred was the largest I'd ever seen or heard of. About two years out of college, I came across a book by Elmer Towns called *The Ten Largest Sunday Schools and What Makes Them Grow*. I remember reading the first chapter and thinking, *Wait. This church has more than five hundred people in it*. I didn't even know such a thing existed! The same was true of the next church in the book, and the next. Each of the ten churches in the book had more than five hundred people in it. The book started to change the way I thought. I suddenly had models of growth beyond anything I'd ever seen.

What's Holding You Back?

I bet you want to achieve more. And you probably love the idea of increasing your potential. But do you still have doubts? If you wanted to, you could find plenty of reasons *not* to strive for your potential. Maintaining the status quo is easier. But that shouldn't stop you. Trying to build your life without removing your limitations and increasing your potential is like building a car in a small shed and being unwilling to knock out the wall to get the car out on the road. Remove the limitations, and the world is open to you.

You have great value. You have great potential. You have the ability to achieve greater significance in your life. It starts with developing self-awareness. More specifically, you need to become aware of the caps of your life and recognize which caps you can't remove and which ones you can.

Once you know what caps you *can* remove, I want to show you *how* to remove them. I want you to become more successful and significant. I'd like to help you reach your potential and achieve your dream. You may be thinking, *You don't even know me!* That's true. I don't know the specifics of your story. But I know that as a human being, you have huge potential. Every person does, so that means *you* do. You specifically.

You may be facing challenges. Others may not believe in you. You may have a tough past. That doesn't take away what you can do or who you can become. The way your life has gone up to now? It doesn't matter. I want to help you believe in yourself and give you a path forward to increasing all of the potential you have.

Write a new story with your life. Hold on to hope as you turn the page, and let's get ready to get to work.

Awareness Questions

1. What is your strategy for developing greater self-awareness? Who will you enlist to help you learn, change, and grow?

2. What are the birth and life caps that you cannot change? List them.

3. What caps have others put on you that you want to remove? What caps have you put on yourself that are limiting your capacity? What must you do to begin loosening those caps?

PART I

ABILITY: DEVELOP THE POTENTIAL YOU ALREADY POSSESS

We often talk about *potential* in the singular. But what if we're thinking about potential the wrong way? Thinking of potential as one thing is too limiting.

In this section I want to talk to you about how we can make the most of the abilities we have. You have dozens, maybe even hundreds. Each area of potential is based on your talents and choices. Right now, I want to focus on the top seven that rely more on talent than choice, though both are involved:

Energy Potential—Your Ability to Push On Physically
Emotional Potential—Your Ability to Manage Your Emotions
Thinking Potential—Your Ability to Think Effectively
People Potential—Your Ability to Build Relationships

Creative Potential—Your Ability to See Options and
Find Answers

Production Potential—Your Ability to Accomplish
Results

Leadership Potential—Your Ability to Lift and Lead
Others

By continually maximizing today's potential in these
areas, which are significant to a person's success, you
will increase tomorrow's potential.

Before we dive into each specific area, I want to say
one more thing about them. They don't develop in iso-
lation. They work together. It may be helpful to think
about this idea in two ways. First, your areas of potential
build in layers. This creates a great foundation for your
life. It's like constructing a house on solid rock instead
of building it on soft sand. It can carry weight. You can
create a large, weighty structure that has the ability to
stand for a long time.

Second, your areas of potential connect to one
another. Each time you increase one area, it has the
opportunity to synergize with another area. For example, if you increase your energy potential so that you can
push on physically, and you increase your leadership
potential, which is the ability to lift and lead others, your
overall effectiveness increases. Where you once ran out
of energy and stopped engaging with people when you

really needed to, you'll learn to push through and be at your best as you interact with them.

As you develop your seven core areas of potential, explore your options. Look for ways to expand your abilities. You will be amazed by the compounding effect you experience.

1

Energy Potential—Your Ability to Push On Physically

There are many capacities that we can increase, but there's nothing we can do to expand time. The number of minutes in a day, days in a week, and weeks in a year are set. Even our time here on earth is fixed. Our days are numbered. That's why we need to focus on our energy. That's something we can influence. If we want to get more done and make a greater impact on the world, we need to increase our energy potential.

Over the years I've noticed that people who reach their potential do not sit back and wait for things to happen to them. They go out and make things happen. That takes energy. It also takes a sense of purpose and focus. Focus your energy by using the three Rs to prioritize:

Requirement—what you have to do

Return—what you do well
Reward—what you love to do

Doing what rewards you almost always gives you energy. The same is true for doing what gives you a high return. However, for most people, fulfilling requirements is not energizing—unless those requirements line up with returns and rewards. If you have the power to align all three of those, you'll always be energized by your work.

You can change jobs. You can talk to your boss and see if what's required of you can be adjusted. Or you can learn to distinguish between what *has* to be done for the organization and what *only you* can do for it. Not everything that has to be done has to be done *by you*. If something is necessary but you don't have to do it personally, delegate it. If it is unnecessary, maybe you have the power to remove it from your requirements entirely.

Even if you don't have the power to change what's required of you on the job, there are still ways to maximize your energy. If you can answer the following five questions and take action based on your answers, you'll see your energy rise dramatically.

1. The Plugged-In Question—"When Am I Fully Charged?"

I wish more people were as intentional about plugging in personally as they are about plugging in their phones and laptops to recharge. If they were, they'd see new levels of productivity and satisfaction in their lives.

So what charges you up? A few of the things that boost my energy include investing in my family and friends, adding value to others, and taking good care of myself physically. What's on your list? If you don't know, then take some time to figure it out. That way, you can be intentional about becoming fully charged.

2. The Depletion Question—"What Wears Me Down?"

Some of us were raised believing that we could accomplish *anything* as long as we tried hard enough. But that's not true. While I believe our potential is unlimited, I also recognize that we cannot excel in areas where we have no talent. No matter how hard I try, I cannot become a professional ballet dancer.

Gallup has proven with their studies on disengagement in the workplace that the anything-is-possible myth has led to many people spending years fighting uphill battles by doing what they're not good at. That's exhausting. Why spend your life trying to be what you're not, instead of trying to be more of who you are naturally? Why not figure out what your natural strengths are and develop those for the benefit of yourself and others? It's the difference between swimming with the current and swimming against it. The first increases your speed and effectiveness while the second depletes your energy. The first makes you shine. The second makes you have to grind. If you grind away in areas of weakness, you'll just get worn out. However, if you shine in your strengths *and* have the strength and tenacity of a grinder, you'll go far.

Another thing that wears most people down is dealing with change. It takes mental, emotional, and physical energy to create change. And the will and discipline needed to sustain change are resources that are more limited than most people realize.

What depletes you? Do you know? Have you paid attention to what sucks the life out of you? Do you avoid those things? It's important to recognize what depletes your energy and take action to defend against them.

3. The Proximity Question—"How Accessible Are My Energy Pluses?"

I discovered the Proximity Principle right after I graduated from college. That June, Margaret and I got married and moved 250 miles away from home. I was ecstatic to start my new life with Margaret, but within a couple of weeks I realized how much energy I had always received from my parents. My dad's positive attitude and confidence were contagious, and as a young person, I was energized whenever I was around him. My mom loved me unconditionally and was always ready to listen to me. In those days there were no cell phones, long-distance calls were expensive, and Margaret and I had no money. So we had very limited contact with my parents. That was quite an adjustment for me, because my energy level went down dramatically.

People are not the only energy pluses we have in our lives. Almost anything can boost your energy as long as it touches you in a positive way. The key is being intentional about keeping those things in proximity to you. You need to figure out what lifts you up. Look at these categories and see if any of them might be possible energy sources for you:

Music—the songs that lift you
Thoughts—the ideas that speak to you
Experiences—the activities that rejuvenate you
Friends—the people who encourage you
Recreation—the fun events that invigorate you
Soul food—the spiritual exercises that strengthen you
Hopes—the dreams that inspire you
Home—the family members who care for you
Giftedness—the talents that activate you
Memories—the recollections that make you smile
Books—the messages that change you

If you discover the things that are energy pluses for you, I think you'll be amazed by how much your energy capacity can increase.

4. The 100 Percent Question—"When Do I Need to Be Full of Energy?"

It's vital to increase your energy as much as possible. It's also crucial to use the energy you have wisely. Use it when you need it, and conserve it when you don't. And know the difference between the two. You need to know when it's showtime every day in your life. No matter what hour of the day it occurs or how often it occurs on a particular day, at those times you need to show up and give 100 percent of your energy. That's the only way you'll maximize your potential.

5. The Margin Question—"Where Is the Space for the Unexpected?"

You need to know the margin you have in your life. By "margin," I mean extra time to breathe, think, and make adjustments. Not only does margin provide space for you to grow, but it also gives you the opportunity to recharge.

I have to confess, this is a continual challenge for me. I'm weak when it comes to creating margin. For too many years I have overscheduled myself. The good news is that I am highly productive. The bad news is that I lose opportunities because I have no margin.

Do you give yourself space in your schedule for the unexpected as well as to recover psychologically and emotionally? In *The Touch of the Earth*, Jean Hersey writes, "It's extremely important not to have one's life all blocked out, not to have the days and weeks totally organized. It's essential to leave gaps and interludes for spontaneous action, for it is often in spontaneity and surprises that we open ourselves to the unlimited opportunities and new areas brought into our lives by chance." Those gaps allow us to use our energy more wisely.[1]

How much have you thought about your energy capacity? Have you assumed that your energy capacity is fixed, that you can't change it? If so, you need to change your mind-set. Start paying close attention to what increases or decreases your energy and begin making adjustments to what you do. Reduce the energy depleters as much as you can. Tap into things that increase your energy capacity. And manage your energy for the things that matter most to you. Trust me—it will change your life.

Energy Potential Questions

1. What are the activities, people, tasks, and places that sap your energy?

2. What are the activities, people, tasks, and places that give you greater energy?

3. In what areas of your life are you not maximizing your energy and the energy of the people around you?

2

Emotional Potential—Your Ability to Manage Your Emotions

Emotional potential is the ability to handle adversity, failure, criticism, change, and pressure in a positive way. All of these things create stress in our lives. I've found that the inability to deal with stress or emotional pressure takes out a lot of people. They give up, break down, or do unhealthy things to try to escape the pressure. However, emotionally strong people are able to manage their emotions and process through difficulties. That allows them to increase their capacity and moves them closer to reaching their full potential.

If your emotional capacity isn't high, this chapter will help you to increase it. If your emotional capacity is naturally high, then perhaps you can use these tips to help others on your team or in your family, because:

- Most people do not see themselves as they really are.
- Many people don't want to resolve their problems; they just want someone to listen to them talk.
- Some people are not emotionally strong, and as a result, they do not cope well with life's difficulties.

I've known and talked to a lot of people who have a high emotional capacity, and I've observed what they do. If you can adopt the following seven traits that I've observed in emotionally strong people, you will increase your emotional capacity.

1. Emotionally Strong People Are Proactive in Dealing with Their Emotions

Emotionally strong people take an active approach to their emotions. They never say, "That's just how I feel. I can't help that." They are never victims of their own feelings. You *can* do things to influence your own emotions. Maybe you can't control them completely, but you can change them through your actions.

All of us are hit in the gut by unwanted surprises, blindsided by negative relationships, and knocked down by blows we didn't see coming. There are times when we want to tell the world how unfair life is. But only by taking action can we pull ourselves out of the pits we find ourselves in. Hoping, wishing, denying, crying, cussing, fussing, moaning, blaming, and waiting only keep us in the pit. The faster we can recover from the shock of the emotion, process it, and move toward action, the quicker our recovery will be and the more emotionally strong we will become. The choice is always ours. We either continually work on mastering our emotions or we are continually mastered by them.

2. Emotionally Strong People Do Not Waste Time Feeling Sorry for Themselves

You can't complain and get ahead at the same time. Moaning about your troubles and moving in the right direction rarely happen together. The way you deal with difficulties and avoid feeling sorry for yourself can be as unique as you are.

I love the way PGA pro golfer Richard Lee handles adversity on the course. "Early in my career my mother-in-law could see how when I had a bad shot, I would get really disappointed. And my negative emotions would start to fill my mind and hurt my play.

"One day she said to me, 'Richard, you will always have days when you make bad shots. Every golfer does. As you walk toward your ball you have a decision to make: Will I dread seeing the lie of my ball and begin filling my mind with negative thoughts and my body with negative emotions? Or will I welcome the ball and be glad I am a golfer and realize that I have an opportunity to make a great recovery shot? If you always welcome the ball regardless of your lie, you will more often make good recovery shots.'"

In life, every one of us is faced with "bad lies." What will be our response when things are not working out, when bad breaks come our way, and when life isn't fair? What will be our mind-set as we "find our ball"? We can let the bad lie ruin our attitude, or we can welcome the ball. If you can ask yourself, "What is the worst that can happen?" and then prepare to accept it, you can hit a good "recovery shot." If it's as bad as the worst, you can deal with it. If it's not as bad as you anticipated, then all the better.

3. Emotionally Strong People Do Not Allow Others to Control Their Relationships

When I began my career as a leader, I thought being effective meant making everyone happy with me. I was a people pleaser, which meant that other people's behavior was really in control of my life. Then one day one of my mentors, Elmer Towns, told me something that really got my attention: "John, the weaker person usually controls the relationship." He went on to explain that emotionally strong people usually have the ability to adjust to difficult relationships, while the weaker person can't or won't.

to stop, figure out why their efforts aren't getting positive results, and change course.

One of the ways successful people keep their emotional potential high is by avoiding falling into this trap. Sure, they make mistakes. But they take the time to learn from them. They don't follow the old rule of business, which says, "When it's over, it's over." Instead, they follow a different rule: it's not over until you've learned from it.

6. Emotionally Strong People Don't Allow the Highs or Lows to Control Their Lives

Every day contains both positives and negatives. You probably know that you shouldn't let the negatives take you down too low, because that can lead to discouragement. But are you also aware that you shouldn't let your highs take you too high?

Successes have a tendency to make us complacent. We start to assume that everything will automatically stay good, so we are tempted to rest on our laurels and try to protect what we have. We can begin to feel entitled, lose perspective, and stop working hard. In the end, both highs and lows have the ability to rob us of reality and limit our activity.

How do I do limit the impact of my highs and lows? I limit the effect of any emotional high or low to the twenty-four-hour period that follows the occurrence. If

I have a great success, I celebrate for twenty-four hours. My team and I give each other high fives, we relive the victory, we compliment one another, but only for a day. Then we get back to work. We know that yesterday's success won't bring us tomorrow's success. *Today's work does.*

Similarly, if I experience a great failure, I allow myself twenty-four hours to feel bad, sing the blues, wear black, and grieve. Toward the end of my emotional time limit, I begin doing things that will bring me back to a level of emotional stability. I spend time with a positive friend. Play a round of golf. Share with someone the lessons I learned in my downtime. Focus on the good things in my life. Or help someone.

Action is the key. Whether dealing with highs or lows, taking action helps you to get back on track and regain control of your emotions. That's how you stay emotionally strong.

7. Emotionally Strong People Understand, Appreciate, and Grow through Their Struggles

Many people resist change, want immediate results, and hope for a life devoid of problems. However, those desires make a person emotionally weak. Why? Because life involves struggle. Emotionally strong people expect difficulties and learn to appreciate the growth they bring. Emotionally strong people do not expect immediate results. As they approach life, they know they are in it for the long haul. As they face struggles, they do so with energy and fortitude. They understand that genuine success takes time. They try new things and fail. They run into obstacles but persevere. They keep going, keep working. They focus on the right decisions they need to make and make them quickly. They realize that they may change their direction overnight, but they won't arrive at their destination overnight. They keep their eyes on the big picture, and they don't quit.

We can't hold on to old emotional baggage and remain emotionally resilient at the same time. Being an emotionally strong person who has high emotional capacity is about being able to start fresh every day and function with a clean slate emotionally.

Emotional Potential Questions

1. In the past, have you considered yourself to be emotionally strong or emotionally weak? Why?

2. Which of the seven practices of emotionally strong people are you best at doing?

3. Which of the seven practices of emotionally strong people is most difficult for you and why? What could you do to improve in that area?

3

Thinking Potential—Your Ability to Think Effectively

Success in achieving goals certainly requires action. But a bias for action has its limits. I discovered a long time ago that if I wanted to increase my overall success capacity, then I needed to increase my thinking potential.

Here is the process that I use to expand ideas and improve my thinking on a daily basis. If you can learn this process, it will make your thinking more thorough. As your thinking improves, the number of good ideas you have will increase. And as you take action on those ideas, your life will become better. Great lives are created by taking good actions on great ideas.

1. Think the Thought—Value Your Thinking

Most people do not recognize the value of good thinking. They have thoughts, but they let them go and don't do anything with them. However, when you value good thoughts, it makes all of your thinking more valuable. That is the starting point of increasing your thinking potential.

Because I value good thinking, I am constantly asking myself questions to help me discover and develop ideas, such as:

Where Can I Find an Idea?

Becoming a better thinker means having the right mindset. Two people can see the same things, go through the same experiences, have the same conversations, yet one walks away with a flurry of great thoughts and the other without a single new idea. To increase your thinking capacity, you need to become an idea digger. *Always* look for ideas and try to mine them.

How Can I Use It?

A lot of people come across an idea and recognize that it's a good idea, yet they don't do anything with it. They don't follow through. That's a shame, because ideas are like muscles. You use them or lose them. When you get a good idea, you need to think to yourself, *How can I use it?*

How Can I Maximize the Idea?

There isn't a single idea that starts out as good as it can be. Every idea can be taken to another level and applied in a way that maximizes it. Any time you have an idea, you should take note of it and plan to give it more thought. Ask yourself, "Where can I maximize that idea?"

If an idea will help your organization, apply it there. Also ask yourself if the idea meets you where you are in your life journey, if it will help you become better in one of your strengths, or if it will help you to grow and get better. When you get one of those ideas, pay attention and prepare to go to step two.

2. Write Out Your Thought—Clarify Your Thinking

University president and United States senator S. I. Hayakawa believed that "learning to write is learning to think. You don't know anything clearly unless you can state it in writing." I think there's a lot of truth to that. Writing makes you think things through. It forces you to articulate the thought. And it makes your thoughts visual.

That doesn't make it easy. Nobel Prize–winning novelist Ernest Hemingway is famous for saying how bad the first draft of anything is. It may take you multiple tries to write something coherent. I know that was usually true for me when I started my writing career. When I wrote my first book, *Think on These Things,* I threw away ten pages for every one I kept. But trust me: putting your ideas down on paper will be worth the effort.

3. Find a Place to Keep Your Thoughts—Capture Your Thinking

Do you know what people's number one time waster is? It's looking for things that are lost. That's why you need a good system for capturing your ideas. And it's why my first goal when I have a good thought is not to lose it. Whether you use your computer, a notebook, or your phone, capture your thoughts—so you can find them again.

I also want to encourage you to designate a place to *find* your thoughts. You need to condition yourself to think in certain places. It doesn't matter where it is—just pick your place and spend time there, and good thoughts will show up. When you have a designated place for something, whatever it is, there is the sense within you that it needs to be filled. And you'll find yourself doing what it takes to fill it. That holds true for your thinking.

4. Rethink Your Thought—Evaluate Your Thinking

This step is perhaps the most critical one in the thinking process, because this is where you cull the bad thoughts and set the good ones on track to be improved and become great ideas. Have you ever awakened in the middle of the night with an idea? It happens to me all the time. In the light of day, most of my midnight ideas are not worth pursuing. But that's OK. The only thing worse than not having a way to capture great ideas, and thus missing them, is capturing a bad idea and trying to make it work. If it's not good, let it go.

Most of the time, I have pretty good instincts about whether an idea is any good. The good ones still speak to me after twenty-four hours. The bad ones don't. If you're not certain how to evaluate an idea, ask yourself these questions:

- Does the thought still speak to me?
- Will this thought speak to others?
- How, where, and when can I use this thought?
- Who can I help by delivering or implementing the thought?

If you don't have positive answers, the idea's probably not worth taking to the next step of the thinking process.

5. Verbalize the Thought—Express Your Thinking

To get the most out of an idea, you need not only to think it through and write it down, but also to talk it out. Both are necessary, but the order in which you do them depends on how you're wired. Here's why:

TALKING EXPRESSES YOUR HEART

Writing about an idea gives your thinking intellectual weight. It creates clarity in your thinking. Talking about an idea gives it emotional weight. It connects your thinking to your heart. Have you ever noticed that you can think about a tragic time from your past pretty rationally, but when you try to tell someone else about it, you become flooded with emotion and get choked up? That's the heart connection that occurs when you express those ideas.

TALKING EXPANDS YOUR IDEA

Many times when you try to elaborate on an idea verbally, you expand it. You give it greater life and clarification. Some of that comes from having to express it. Some comes from the nonverbal feedback you receive from listeners when they don't understand what you're saying. Some comes from answering questions people ask you about your idea. All of these things help you improve your idea. They also help you expand your thinking capacity for the future.

Are you wired as a natural talker or a natural thinker? Start with whichever comes naturally to you. But be sure to include both solo thinking time and time talking with others to get the best out of your thinking capacity.

6. Put the Thought on the Table—Share Your Thinking

I want to encourage you to share your thinking with others to take it to another level. To do that, follow these steps:

• **Bring a good thought to the table.** It doesn't have to be a great thought, but it needs to be a good one.

• **Share your desire for others to improve on your thought.** You need to want better thoughts more than you want the credit.

• **Ask everyone to participate.** People should know that they're either at the table or on the menu.

• **Ask questions.** Nothing stimulates improved thinking more than questions.

• **Let the best idea win.** When the best idea wins, you win!

When you bring a good thought to the table with a small group of good thinkers, they will always make your thought better. Just make sure you bring good thinkers to the table and, as my friend Linda Kaplan Thaler says, make sure you have at least one person who can recognize a great idea. Do that, and you'll always walk away with a better idea.

7. Practice the Thought—Take Your Thinking for a Walk

Once an idea has been put on the table and improved by a key group of people, it's time to take the idea out and let more people see it. I think of this as being like taking a dog for a walk in the park. People see it, react to it, and make comments.

You learn a lot when you present an idea to people who don't know you or who won't automatically give you the benefit of the doubt. If the only person who ever hears your ideas is your mother, you'll think all of them are good. Present them to strangers and skeptics, and you'll find out where you really stand. It's always easier to think an idea than to practice it. An idea always sounds better when it hasn't been challenged. But an unchallenged idea is rarely able to live in the real world. That's why you need to take it for a walk and see what happens.

8. Question the Thought—Expand Your Thinking

Earlier, I explained that we need to evaluate our thoughts by asking ourselves if they still speak to us after twenty-four hours have passed. But it's important at this stage for us to question our thinking again.

After practicing a thought, ask yourself, "What did I learn from practicing it?" to judge whether the idea is still viable. We should never be so in love with a thought that we don't question it.

The process of questioning expands your thinking, your capacity, and your potential. You'll discover a few things you should do and a half-dozen or more things you shouldn't. And you'll be better for having gone through the painful process.

9. Embrace the Thought—Own Your Thinking

Something powerful happens when a person moves from *believing* in an idea to *owning* an idea. Believing in an idea can be good, but it's very limiting. When you *believe* in an idea, it's like investing in an endeavor with someone else's money. You give it a try and you hope it works. However, when you *own* an idea, it's like putting your own money into an investment. You do what it takes to make it work. The greater the investment, the more you feel that it *has to work*.

10. Launch the Thought—Implement Your Thinking

When you launch an idea, you need to be clear about what you want people to know and what you want people to do. The launch is the greatest test of any idea. The implementation demonstrates an idea's real value—or lack of value. When it works, it's powerful, because everyone sees it.

11. Land the Thought—Make Your Thinking Work

Launching an idea is very rewarding. But the results come with the landing. It's similar to the way gymnastics are scored. At a meet, the tumbling passes and the aerial vaults of the best gymnasts always gets lots of oohs and aahs from the audience, but their twists and turns in the air don't bring high scores unless the athletes stick their landings.

The landing always matters.

12. Upgrade the Thought—Mature Your Thinking

When a thought lands and makes a positive difference, the temptation is to celebrate and move on. I'm all for celebrating. Wins can be hard to come by, and when we do experience a win, we should thank the people who helped to make it happen and give them the credit they deserve. But if we do that without looking for a way to upgrade the thought, we miss a great opportunity. Growth requires your thoughts to be continually upgraded.

If you want to increase your potential, maximize your capacity, and be successful, develop your thinking. High thinking capacity and the ability to sustain your thinking will give you a higher return than being smart or working hard. The difference between average thinkers and good thinkers is like the difference between ice cubes and icebergs. Ice cubes are small and short-lived. Icebergs are huge, and there is much more to them than meets the eye. Their potential is enormous.

Thinking Potential Questions

1. Do you have a system for capturing your ideas? If so, how well is it working for you? If not, what could you do to begin recording your ideas so you don't lose them?

2. Who are the people you bring to the table to improve your ideas? How much are they helping you? What can you change to get them to help you more?

3. Do you have a greater bias toward action or toward thinking? What would happen if you were able to harness both?

4

People Potential—Your Ability to Build Relationships

In 2004 I wrote a book called *Winning with People* out of the conviction that people can usually trace their successes and failures to the relationships in their lives. We are defined by our relationships.

Maybe up until now your relationships haven't been as positive, rewarding, and productive as you'd like them to be. That's OK, because you can learn how to build better relationships and increase your relational potential. I've spent some time thinking about the things I've done that have enabled me to establish and enjoy long-term relationships, and these seven steps can help you to develop stronger relationships with others.

1. Care about People Every Day

You cannot increase your people capacity unless you value people and care about them. If you don't like people, don't respect them, and don't believe they have value, it stands as a barrier to your success with them. You can't secretly look down on others and build them up at the same time. However, if you truly care about people, it shows. And it makes the development of positive relationships possible.

2. Make Yourself More Valuable in Your Relationships

What's the fastest way to make a relationship better? Make *yourself* better so that you have more to give. That requires an abundance mind-set. That's the belief that there's more than enough for everyone and people always have the potential to find or create more.

Try improving yourself and your situation with the purpose of giving to others and see what happens. As you give, I guarantee that your ability to give more will increase. It will motivate you to give more of your thoughts, time, assets, relationships, influence, and giftedness.

I ask a lot of questions to discover how I can better add value to others. There is no better way to show people you value them than by asking for their opinion. Communicating is about adding value to people, not adding value to yourself. The more you know about people and the more you improve yourself, the more you can make a difference in the lives of others. You can give more value to others, and that increases your relational capacity.

3. Put Yourself in Their World

Are you familiar with the saying, "It's lonely at the top"? I don't like it. It's a sign of disconnection. I tell leaders that if they're lonely at the top, it means no one is following them. They need to get off their mountain or out of their ivory tower, go to where their people are, and spend time with them. People don't care how much you know until they know how much you care.

Make yourself available to the people in your life. And be alert to ways you can go to them when they need it. Sometimes you don't even need to say a word. Just be there. Just let others know what they mean to you.

4. Focus Your Relationships on Benefiting Others, Not Yourself

To build great relationships, you need to want more *for* people than you want *from* people. The people who want more for others and give more than they take are pluses. The ones who want and take more than they give are minuses. That's simple relational math. I determined that I wanted to be a plus with people. With those closest to me, I want to be a plus *plus*. My desire is to make five relational deposits for every relational withdrawal I make from the relationship. I don't always succeed, but it is my goal.

I never want to take any relationship for granted. I never want to assume that a relationship gives me privileges that are not mine. Assumption is a killer in relationships. It needs to be replaced with *awareness*. If you want to increase your relational capacity, you should be continually aware that relationships never stay the same. They never stay alive on their own. They need cultivation. And you have to keep being intentional about adding value to continue being a plus in another person's life.

5. Be a Consistent Friend in Your Relationships

I believe the ability to be a good friend is something that is often undervalued and overlooked today. Good relationships are built upon consistency. Relationships that are volatile and continually up and down are not easy. They provide no relational "rest." There is nothing pleasant about being in relationships that are continually high-maintenance. You can't be good friends with people when someone has to walk on eggshells or when any conversation could lead to the end of the relationship.

We must be dependable and consistent. We must be trustworthy. Our friends must know that they can depend on us. How? These tips have helped me over the years:

BELIEVE THE BEST ABOUT PEOPLE

Try to see people as they could be, not necessarily as they are. When you believe the best of people, you don't feel the need to correct them or try to fix them. Believing the best of others is always the right thing to do, even if it means you may not always be right. People are more apt to change when another person believes in them than when people *don't* believe in them.

DON'T ALLOW OTHER PEOPLE'S BEHAVIOR TO CONTROL YOU

Too often people allow the actions of others to impact their own attitudes and emotions. They let others' inconsistency make them inconsistent. But you need to understand that when that happens, you've allowed it. As humans we have the capacity to create and control our own attitudes and emotions. We need to make that choice for ourselves every day. Otherwise, people will control us.

PLACE HIGH VALUE ON RELATIONSHIPS, EVEN IN DIFFICULT SITUATIONS

Dealing with people is sometimes difficult. As a leader, I have occasionally had to fire an individual. Letting someone go may be the right thing to do for the organization, but we should also make sure to do the right thing for the person relationally. If possible, I seek to continue the relationship. Sometimes the person doesn't want that. That's OK. I cannot determine what they are going to do. I can only determine what I am going to do, and what I will do is remain a friend to them.

UNCONDITIONALLY LOVE PEOPLE

Unconditional love is the greatest gift we can give another person. It allows someone to feel secure, be vulnerable, sense their worth, and discover who they really are. I believe that all people long to have a consistent friend who loves them, believes in them, and is continually there for them no matter the circumstances. If you're willing to be that kind of person for others, not only will it expand your people capacity, it will also give you a more satisfying life.

You may be thinking, *I can't do this with everyone, because some people are just difficult.* That's true—for all of us. In the end, our goal should be to treat others better than they treat us, to add value to them in a greater capacity than maybe they expect.

6. Create Great Memories for People

It has been my observation that most people do not maximize the experiences they have in life. To do so, two things are essential: intentionality on the front end of the experience and reflection on the back end. So anytime you can help people to do those things, the experience becomes special for them, and it often creates a positive memory for them.

Most of us have traditions and memories associated with special days, but I want to challenge you to make memories out of everyday experiences. Every time you are with people, ask yourself these questions:

- What can I say that will affirm those with me?
- What question can I ask that they will find interesting to discuss?
- What can we do that will be different and fun?
- What do I know that they would want to know?
- Do I have a secret of my own that I can tell them?

All of these can lead to great memories. Many little things done repeatedly with high intention are better than big things done only occasionally. You can make big or small moments special for others, but you have to be intentional about it.

7. Move toward the Relationships You Desire in Your Life

Put yourself in a position to meet and spend time with the right people. I always want to spend time with people who know more than I do, and whenever I'm with someone I respect and have gotten to know, I ask them, "Who do you know that I should know?" That question has given me a greater return in life than any other. The greatest way to know whom you should know is to ask someone who knows you.

I want to encourage you to be intentional and show initiative by moving toward the relationships you desire in life. If you wait for the right people to meet you, you won't meet the right people. I don't wait for all the stars to align before I take action, and neither should you. Find one star and start moving toward it.

Whom do you know who knows someone you should know? You may be only one person away from the next big thing that you need in your life. You may be thinking, *I'm not a people person.* If that's true, ask people with strong relational skills to help you. Let them complement and complete you. You can draw people to you by saying to them, "I need you."

The more you value people, put yourself into their world, seek to add value to them, and be their friend, the better your life will be. Not only that, but doing these things will increase your people capacity, improve your potential, and improve your life. Just remember, helping people is always worth the effort.

People Potential Questions

1. When you interact with people, where is your focus? Are you usually thinking about how you can help

them or how they can help you? What must you do to make benefiting others the focus of your relationships?

2. Which of the people in your life would describe you as a consistent friend? Which would not? What must you change to become a consistently positive friend to everyone?

3. What relationship do you desire to move toward to improve your life and capacity? What is the first step you must take to facilitate the connection?

5

Creative Potential—Your Ability to See Options and Find Answers

Is it true that some people are born highly creative? Of course. There are the rare few who breathe to create and are gifted with the ability to change the world in that regard. In fact, some argue that all of us are born creative but most of us lose that creativity as we grow up. But you can rekindle the creativity that's already in you, plus cultivate new pathways of creativity.

I want to walk you through the eight keys to increasing creative potential that I've used to go from bottom of the class to top of my game. Embrace each of them and you will immediately see an increase in your ability to see options, solve problems, and find answers.

1. Believe There Is *Always* an *Answer*

Why are creative people willing to give time, patience, and experimentation to "unsolvable" problems? Because creativity always takes time, patience, and experimentation. You just have to enter into the process believing there is an answer. Creativity is a mind-set. You have to believe that answers and solutions are out there if you're willing to keep fighting to find them. Each door you open leads to another door. *One* of those doors will eventually lead to an answer.

2. Believe There Is *More Than One* *Answer*

My favorite word is *options*. However, that has not always been true. In my younger years I was always quick to give people what I thought was *the* answer to any question they asked. I was confident, opinionated, and certain about everything. Today I think broadly and search for as many possible answers as I can find. Only when I develop a long list of options do I line them up and ask, "What is the *best* option?" I take great comfort in finding several effective ways to get things accomplished and seek to discover as many options as possible.

If you're a leader, you may want to adopt a practice that I've used with my staff. Whenever people on my team come to me with a problem, I ask them to prepare at least three solutions to that problem. I do that to help them to become more creative, more open-minded, and more willing to consider different ideas and opinions. If they can become flexible and demonstrate the ability to adapt to fluctuating situations, they will be more effective and productive. I know from my own experience that I became more creative when I began to believe there was always an answer. That creativity multiplied dramatically when I discovered that there are many answers.

3. Believe That Everything and Everyone Can Get Better

Creative people, whether they are artists, inventors, businesspeople, or teachers, believe there are always better ways to do things. And they search for them. When you believe that everyone and everything can get better, it gives you confidence that you can help people and make a difference. And it inspires you to keep looking for ways to solve problems and pursue opportunities.

4. Understand That Questions Help You to Be More Creative

Questions always spur creativity. Why? Because questions cause you to explore, to seek out. The phrase "what if" is one of my favorites because it's the start of a question that will lead to sometimes breathtakingly creative answers. Here are some questions to ask yourself to help you to become more creative:

HOW CAN I MAKE THINGS BETTER?

If you're already successful, this is a fantastic question to ask. Anytime we're successful, there is a temptation to be lulled into a feeling of false security, to believe that we have arrived. But the greatest detriment to continual success is relying on past success.

WHAT CAN I DO TO BECOME BETTER?

I am obsessed with becoming better every day. I don't spend time thinking about any honors I've been given in the past. I'm grateful, but I also recognize that awards are given for what we've done yesterday. The question I ask myself is, "What am I doing today?"

ARE THE RIGHT PEOPLE AT THE TABLE?

The people around you make all the difference when it comes to creativity. You need people who are willing to prepare as well as to dream. And you need people who are willing to be as tenacious as you are in searching for answers.

HOW CAN I CONNECT THINGS WITH CREATIVITY?

As Steve Jobs said, "Creativity is just connecting things. When you ask creative people how they did something, they feel a little guilty because they didn't really do it;

they just saw something. It seemed obvious to them after a while." If you want to increase your creativity, begin looking for connections.

5. Be Comfortable with Half-Baked Ideas

When I was young, I held on to ideas way too long before I shared them with others. Why? I wanted them to be "presentable." I didn't want to fail. I didn't want my ideas to be rejected. And I wanted credit. Back then, looking good was more important to me than getting good.

Today I'm in love with half-baked ideas and am willing to ask for them as well as share them with others. Why? Because when we do, we gain at least these three benefits:

WE INCREASE OUR ODDS OF BEING SUCCESSFUL

If you want to accomplish many things, you have to try many things—even if you feel they're not quite ready. Dan Ariely, Duke University professor and author of *Irrationally Yours: On Missing Socks, Pick-up Lines, and Other Existential Puzzles,* says that if you try thirty new things this year, you might find that you rack up fifteen good experiences. But if you wait to try things only when you're sure of success, you might experience only three good things.

WE GAIN MORE PRACTICE WITH CREATIVE IDEAS

Keeping our imaginations sharp is essential to creative thinking and problem-solving. That requires practice. Unfortunately, as we get older, most people practice creative thinking less and less. We stop using our imaginations. Working with half-baked ideas forces us to use our imaginations and practice creative thinking.

WE BECOME MORE COMFORTABLE WITH OUR MISSES

If you throw a lot of ideas at the wall, some will stick and others won't. And that's good. You can't succeed if you don't try. And once you realize you're no worse off for having tried and failed, it gives you confidence to keep trying.

Creative people fail, and the best fail often. They're like children who try an idea before it's formed, and if it doesn't work, they move on to the next idea. And they keep moving on until they find one that works. If you want to be more creative, get used to missing the mark.

6. Be Comfortable Letting Go of What You Embraced Yesterday

When was the last time you said goodbye to something that you worked hard on but no longer works today? In the beginning, it wasn't quick or easy for me to let go of things. But over time, I have been able to move on and let go because I've learned some lessons:

- **It's easier to let go of something if you're going to get something better.** You don't let go just for the sake of letting go. You let go only because tomorrow looks better than yesterday.
- **People usually cut their losses too late.** My brother Larry, who is a fine businessman, taught me many years ago about cutting losses. He would say, "John, try to let your first loss be your last loss." I haven't always done that well, but I have gotten a lot better.
- **Excellence is possible only with creative dissatisfaction.** If we're satisfied, we don't try to get better. At the other extreme, if we embrace dissatisfaction without a desire for excellence, we just become miserable or depressed. However, when you couple dissatisfaction with the desire for improvement, you become innovative.
- **You can't fall in love with structure.** When your security is structure, rules, and regulations, you stop being creative. You can't love both staying in the box and creativity.

Are you willing to let go of some things you love? If not, you're going to have a hard time being creative and becoming any better than you are today.

7. Ask Creative People to Help You

When you ask creative people to help you, your goal isn't just to have people come together for a creative think session. Your goal is to have the *right* people in the meeting. What are the qualities of the right people? Here is what I look for:

- **Fluency**—the ability to generate a number of ideas so that there is an abundance of possible solutions
- **Flexibility**—the ability to produce many different kinds of ideas in various categories for any given problem
- **Elaboration**—the ability to add to, embellish, or build from an idea
- **Originality**—the ability to create fresh, unique, unusual, or different ideas
- **Complexity**—the ability to drill down and conceptualize difficult, intricate, or multifaceted ideas
- **Boldness**—the willingness be daring, try new things, and take risks
- **Imagination**—the ability to invent, see, and conceptualize ingenious new ideas
- **Security**—the willingness to appreciate others' ideas and not protect their own
- **Values**—the ability to think and create in accordance with my values and priorities

These are the people who can help you create. Leave out analysts, critics, editors, educators, and implementers.

Otherwise the group's creative wings will be clipped before you are ever given any room to fly.

8. Give Yourself Creative Retreats

Solitude is the other side of the coin in creativity. While I love bringing together a group of creative people to brainstorm, I also love spending time by myself, thinking. We need inspiration from within as well as from without.

Creativity flourishes in solitude. There is a relationship between scheduling a time to be creative and being inspired to create. That's why I try to schedule time every day as well as plan extended times weekly, monthly, and yearly.

You will become as creative as the amount of time you set aside for it. If you're like me, you need time alone to think and create for yourself and others. Setting aside that creative time of retreat can give you the greatest ROI—return on investment—in your life.

If you desire to increase your creativity capacity, you can do it. You can train yourself to see possibilities. You can learn to find answers. You can become someone who always offers options. And you can work with others to become inventive and innovative. If you can pair that with productivity, which is the subject of the next chapter, you'll *really* be able to increase your capacity.

Creative Potential Questions

1. When it comes to problems, challenges, and obstacles, do you believe there is *always* a solution? Explain your answer.

2. Do you find it difficult or easy to let go of old successes and solutions? Why? How could you leverage a stronger faith in the future in order to let go of the past?

3. Are you better at pulling together a group of creative people to get ideas or at retreating into solitude to think? What could you do to improve in the area where you currently don't do as well?

The Uphill Climb

Paul grew up in Pittsburgh, Pennsylvania. You know how some people say, "We grew up poor, but we never knew it"? Paul says, "We grew up poor, and we *knew* we were poor. We felt it every day."

Nobody gave Paul much of a chance because he had a speech impediment. Back in those days, the school system treated him like he was disabled. His friends made fun of him and called him stupid. Paul dealt with that by working—delivering papers, collecting bottles, selling light bulbs door-to-door, raking leaves in the fall, and shoveling driveways in the winter. He did whatever he could to make an honest buck to help his family.

By the time he was fifteen, Paul was pretty discouraged with school and decided he'd rather just work. So he dropped out and started work on a roofing crew. But he also joined the Guardian Angels, a group of citizen-volunteers who patrolled the streets to discourage crime.

It took no time at all for Paul to rise up. He quickly recruited a hundred young people into his chapter. He was so good at recruiting and fund-raising that he soon became the number two man in the organization and traveled the country with founder Curtis Sliwa.

Paul enjoyed his role with the Guardian Angels, but after seven years, the entrepreneurial bug bit him again, and at age twenty-two he decided he wanted to start his own cleaning business. For sixteen years, through many ups and downs, Paul led his company, At Your Service, and grew it into a highly profitable business.

While he was learning and growing, Paul decided that he wanted to help others become more successful in their careers. So he started to teach them from a book that had changed his life: *Think and Grow Rich* by Napoleon Hill. He found it so rewarding that he located an organization to train and certify him as a speaker. Within months, he became the most successful entrepreneur in that network of speakers, while still running his cleaning business. The organization's founder discovered this and wanted to hire Paul to run his conference business, so Paul sold At Your Service and changed careers. By then, he had one hundred full-time employees cleaning 150 locations every night, including offices, restaurants, country clubs, movie theaters, imaging centers, hospitals, and even a zoo.

Five years later, he approached me along with mutual friend Scott Fay and said, "John, let's start a world-class coaching company." It was something I'd never considered before. And to be honest, I wasn't sure I wanted to do it. But Paul was very persuasive, and we decided to partner together. I would give the program my name and teach the coaches my values, and Paul would do all the other work.

In just six years, Paul did wonders. He took the John Maxwell Team from zero coaches to more that fifteen thousand coaches. He grew it from his headquarters in south Florida and spread it to 145 countries around the world. As the president of the John Maxwell Team, every day he climbs uphill and leads thousands of certified coaches to climb with him. I've met few people in my life with his ability to produce.

I find Paul's story remarkable. It illustrates the power of perseverance and productivity. Paul found a way, and I want to share that way with you. Paul's principles can be applied to anything you want to make happen, whether it's a business, a nonprofit organization, a home remodel, a sports team—you name it. If you want to increase your production capacity, take the following ideas to heart:

1. Visualize the Perfect Outcome

Do you have a vision for what you want to accomplish? Have you created a mental model of perfection for what you desire to achieve? If not, you need to work on that. It's your starting point. Put as much detail into it as you can. Will it actually *be* perfect? No. But that idea is where you need to start.

2. Start Working before You Know How to Achieve the Vision

When you want to accomplish something, you have to have a vision for what you're trying to do, but you also have to be willing to take action in the face of uncertainty. You need to tap into your thinking capacity to know what you're shooting for, but you also need to have a bias for action to be productive. You have to be willing to take a step, probably a small step.

Most people want to start with one bold, certain leap. They want a big head start, a quantum leap. But Paul points out that there are very few quantum leaps. If we're willing to take one small step, ten small steps, one hundred small steps, then we may have a chance to make a leap later. It may look like an overnight success to others, but we know it's the result of many small successes. And you don't achieve those unless you're willing to take that *first* uncertain step.

3. Fail Fast, Fail First, and Fail Often

This step seems to fly in the face of the idea of striving for perfection. But to be productive, you have to be willing to fail. A lot. A key is to avoid thinking of your efforts as right or wrong, as successes or failures. Instead ask yourself if what you did got you closer to your vision of perfection. If it did, it's a win. If it didn't, then look at what didn't work, make adjustments, and try again immediately.

Are you willing to fail? Are you willing to fail repeatedly? Are you willing to learn from what didn't work? That's what will be required for you to blow the cap off of your production potential.

4. Stay Focused Longer Than Other People Do

Paul learned a lot of lessons as a budding entrepreneur during his childhood. "As I look back," says Paul, "I realize that I stayed focused longer than most people. When all the other kids would go out to shovel snow, most kids would do it for thirty minutes and maybe earn three or four dollars. Then they would quit. I had the ability to stay focused, regardless of the distractions, to the exclusion of outside conditions or circumstances. That was what was giving me the results."

That still gives Paul results. It will give you results, too. Paul started out working hard because people told him he wasn't smart. Now he recognizes how smart he is, but his work ethic is still intact. So I have to ask: How long do you stick with something to make it work? And how hard do you work at it while you're doing it? Do you stay focused? Here's the thing you need to learn from Paul's example. He initiates *many* tries at *one thing,* not *one* try at *many things.* That's an approach anyone can adopt, regardless of talent, intelligence, resources, or opportunity.

5. Take Inventory of Your Skills and Resources

About two years into his cleaning business, Paul hit a wall. "I was doing what I'd been told my whole life," says Paul. "I was told that if I worked hard and did honest work that things would be OK. I was working hard. I was doing honest work, but things weren't OK. I would get a new account, then I would lose two others. I would get an employee well trained, and then he would leave to earn twenty-five or fifty cents an hour more somewhere else. It was the proverbial 'one step forward, two steps back,' and I didn't know how to change it. I was stuck. And let me tell you: stuck stinks."

Back then Paul didn't know how to navigate himself out of his problem. So he started to think about himself and his skills. He realized that he needed to grow. "If you are not growing," Paul says, "you are not living at your full capacity." If you want to be more productive, you need to take charge of your own productivity.

6. Stop Doing What You're Not Great at Doing

You will drastically increase your production capacity if you stop doing what you're not great at and instead focus on what you do best. Find ways to focus your time and attention and work toward eliminating from your schedule anything that doesn't have a high return.

7. Tune In to Your Team Every Day

Because Paul recognizes the importance of the team, he is highly intentional in staying connected to his people. Every day he calls somebody to check in with them or drops into their office just to chat. He pays attention to his team's social media. He wants to know how they're doing. "You've got to know the vibe of the tribe," says Paul.

I do this as well. I try to have dinner with key members of my staff, and I take them with me to events so that we can spend time together. I know that those closest to me determine my level of success, so I want to maintain and develop those relationships and add value to my team members whenever I can. If you want to be productive, you need to develop a team, connect with team members, and keep adding value to them.

8. Make Decisions Every Day to Move Yourself and the Team Forward

When Paul starts any endeavor, his first goal is to just get started and make things functional. For example, when he started the John Maxwell Team, he didn't even have a website. But he didn't let that stop him. He did the things he knew how to do and then worked to make improvements. And that's where he focuses a lot of his production energy. That process requires the ability to make decisions every day.

One of the things I find most interesting about Paul is that he doesn't see decisions as right or wrong, good or bad. He judges only whether or not they move him and the team forward or backward in the journey toward his vision. You will only reach your production capacity if you are willing to make decisions. And Paul's approach to decision-making can free you up.

When it comes to character and ethical decisions, yes, there is right and wrong. But when it comes to productivity and achievement, there isn't. Either something works or it doesn't. Either it takes you forward or it doesn't. If you develop the habit of making quick decisions, try new things, and judge whether or not they take you forward, you will be more productive.

9. Continually Reevaluate What Could Work Better

Productive people are always working to become better and to find better ways of doing things. The place where today and tomorrow meet is where you can create positive change. The only time you really control is now. You can't change yesterday. You can't control tomorrow. But you can choose what you do today with the goal that those choices will make things better tomorrow.

Few things will positively impact your potential or your success more quickly and more thoroughly than increasing your production potential. If you take a cue from Paul, you can do that immediately. Adopt his practices. Repeat them daily until they become habits. And watch what happens.

Production Potential Questions

1. Is your natural inclination to be a historian, who examines the past; a reporter, who observes and comments on the present; or a futurist, who acts today with the intention of improving tomorrow? What could you do to focus more on the emerging future?

2. Using Paul's story as inspiration, how would you describe your vision of a perfect future? What would you be doing? Describe it in as much detail as possible.

3. What downhill habits do you currently possess that are taking you away from that ideal future? What uphill habits must you cultivate to replace the unproductive ones?

7

Leadership Potential—Your Ability to Lift and Lead Others

If you've read some of my other books on leadership, you may be wondering what I plan to teach in this chapter. I'm going to teach you from the new things I am learning now. Some of what I'm going to share are new thoughts layered on older thoughts. Some are old thoughts that have spurred new thoughts. I hope all of them increase your capacity as they have increased mine.

1. Ask Questions and Listen to Understand and Find Your People

Communication is the language of leadership. For years I held on to the illusion that as long as I was talking and giving direction, communication was happening. I was focused on vision. I thought leadership was about me and what I wanted. Today, I want my people to know me, and I want to know them.

Questions open up doors and allow us to connect with others. They place value on the other person. And they give us a different perspective. Before we attempt to *set* things right as leaders, we need to *see* things right. The highest compliment you can give people is to ask them their opinion.

However, none of that works if you don't listen. Questions start the conversation, but listening encourages it to continue. Listening shows that I want to understand someone before I try to be understood by them. Questions + Listening = Quality Conversation. Quality Conversation = Quality Leadership.

2. Connect with People before Asking Them to Change

By its nature, leadership is about creating change. As a leader, you are inviting people to change their focus, change their energy, change their skills, and sometimes even change their direction in life for the sake of the team and the accomplishment of the vision. How do you get people to trust you for so many changes? Trust needs to be built on good relationships, and good relationships start with good connections.

If you're a task-oriented person, connecting may be something you have to work at to achieve. If you're a people person, building the relationships may come naturally. But making the transition from relationship building to movement requires what I call a *leadershift*. That "shift" is the transition from connecting with people to helping them make the changes necessary for the benefit of the team.

One of the keys to helping team members make successful changes is to set expectations for them up front. It increases the odds of positive change later in the relationship. I want to walk you through the six steps I use to set expectations. I believe they will set you up for success as you connect with people and then invite them to change.

LET THEM KNOW YOU VALUE THEM

The greatest gift leaders give team members is their belief in them, letting them know that they are valued. If I as your leader don't value you, I will try to manipulate you for *my* advantage instead of investing in you for *your* advantage.

So in setting expectations for people, I clearly communicate how much I value them as individual people, not just as team members. And that means I care enough for them to confront them. I value them too much to allow them to remain the same. Once they know that my expectations for them are birthed out of how much I value them, the environment has been set for the next step.

IDENTIFY THE VALUE THEY PLACE ON THEMSELVES

Self-worth is foundational to belief. The moment that your belief in yourself goes up, so can your commitment to help yourself. If the people on your team don't believe in themselves, as the leader you need to try to help them find that belief. You need to encourage them. You need to speak positive words of affirmation. You need to teach them. And you need to help them put wins under their belts. Does that always work? No. But if their self-worth never rises, neither will their performance.

TELL THEM GROWTH IS EXPECTED

As a leader, you want your people to grow, and you want them to know it on the front end. If they know you will hold them accountable for growth, the chances of it happening increase dramatically. One of the greatest mistakes leaders make is sharing expectations but failing to later include accountability.

SHOW THEM CHANGE IS ESSENTIAL

It is impossible to get better without making changes. No one has ever stayed the same while at the same time rising to a higher level. Being willing to change is one of the prices we pay to grow. Good leaders help people recognize and accept that price. You can't make the changes for them, but you can show them what needs changing, assist them, and encourage them.

KEEP THE CONNECTION CONSTANT

When it comes to expectations, leaders can never think, *Set it and forget it*. People rarely lead themselves forward or correct themselves when they get off track. People want to be empowered. But often what they need most is accountability. Keeping your connection constant and gently nudging them forward provides both encouragement and consistent accountability.

ASK, "WILL YOU HELP ME HELP YOU?"

When you ask people if they will help you to help them, you are able to measure their level of participation and commitment. By getting them to declare the ways that *they* want help to grow and change, you obtain their full buy-in. And if they don't follow through, you can hold them accountable for what they declared they would do.

3. Demonstrate Transparency before Challenging People

One of the most valuable things you can do to increase your leadership capacity is to be authentic and transparent with people and to share your story, especially before you challenge them to attempt something difficult.

Too many leaders think they have to project a perfect image to have leadership credibility. They think they always have to put their best foot forward. What they don't understand is that their best foot is a flawed foot. They miss the power of their own stories of imperfection. A leader's story of struggle, growth, and improvement can inspire people and change lives. People respect leaders who tell the truth but who still hold fast to the vision and keep leading the team forward.

4. Put Others ahead of Yourself

In the beginning of my career, my leadership was all about me. All I did was wonder, *Does this person want to hear my vision? Does she want to help my team? Does he want to help me? What can this person can do for me?* That changed when my attention began to focus on equipping and empowering others. I want to encourage you to make that same shift from *me* to *we*, if you haven't made it already. Why? I believe these three factors will make you want to change:

REALITY—AS THE CHALLENGE ESCALATES, THE NEED FOR TEAMWORK ELEVATES

Every worthwhile dream is greater than the individual who initially holds it. When we recognize that truth, it motivates us to ask others for help. But we also need to realize that people are most likely to help us *after* we have helped them in some way. When we equip and empower our team, everyone is able to work together to achieve even the largest dream.

MATURITY—WITH ONE TINY EXCEPTION, THE WORLD IS COMPOSED OF OTHERS

I define maturity as unselfishness. It's being able to see things from other people's perspective because you value them. It means building ladders so that others can climb, not fighting to climb the ladder yourself. Effective leadership can never be all about you, because you're not the only one on your team.

PROFITABILITY—MEASURE YOUR SUCCESS BY WHAT YOU GIVE, NOT WHAT YOU GAIN

No matter what you do professionally, you should judge your success by how much you are able to help others. In the end, life is about people. Never forget it. Take care of your people instead of taking care of your career. If you are willing to make success about giving rather than gaining, you will find your life to be greatly rewarding. I know I do. And the people I invest in remind me of why I keep doing it.

I want to ask you a question: What do you want your life to stand for? As you grow old and draw near to the end of your life, what kind of impact do you want to have made on the world? I hope you'll choose to add value to people. And I hope you'll choose to become a leader of higher capacity. The more influence you develop, the greater the positive impact you'll be able to make.

Leadership Potential Questions

1. How much time and effort do you spend on increasing your leadership capacity? What kind of priority has that been for you up until now? If you're willing to make it a higher priority, what will you do to increase it?

2. How well do you connect with people and challenge them? Are you better at one than the other? How can you improve the one you don't do as well?

3. What changes should you make and what specific action could you take to put others ahead of yourself, especially in your leadership?

PART II

CHOICES: DO THE THINGS THAT MAXIMIZE YOUR POTENTIAL

You have the right and the power to choose how much potential you have. Self-awareness is something we learn. Ability is a gift that we already possess. Choices add to both the things we learn and the gifts we possess.

The next ten chapters of this book will help you to maximize your capacity by making choices in ten key areas. These areas aren't skills or talents; they are life choices. The more you live them and learn to love them, the larger your capacity will be and the greater your success.

I want you to know that one of the choices I discuss is spiritual capacity. As a person of faith, I cannot with integrity omit this choice from the book, but I'm aware that you may want to skip that chapter. And that, of course, is fine with me. I value you as a person no matter what. That being said, here are the ten choices:

Responsibility Potential—Your Choice to Take Charge of Your Life

Character Potential—Your Choices Based on Good Values

Abundance Potential—Your Choice to Believe There Is More Than Enough

Discipline Potential—Your Choice to Focus Now and Follow Through

Intentionality Potential—Your Choice to Deliberately Pursue Significance

Attitude Potential—Your Choice to Be Positive Regardless of Circumstances

Risk Potential—Your Choice to Get Out of Your Comfort Zone

Spiritual Potential—Your Choice to Strengthen Your Faith

Growth Potential—Your Choice to Focus on How Far You Can Go

Partnership Potential—Your Choice to Collaborate with Others

As you explore these areas of potential, I want to encourage you to make the choices that will help you to become the person you *can* be. Turn the page to explore the first choice.

8

Responsibility Potential—Your Choice to Take Charge of Your Life

There is nothing sexy or exciting about the word *responsibility*, yet it is the first topic that I want to discuss in this section on choices you can make to maximize your potential. Why? Because it is foundational to most of the other important choices we make in our lives.

All of us have a tendency to blame others for our circumstances and even our choices. We need to overcome that tendency if we want to increase our potential and live a life with no limits. If you're willing to make choices that increase your sense of responsibility, you will see a corresponding increase in your success. Here's why:

1. Responsibility Creates the Foundation for Your Success

When I was a young man just beginning my career, I was eager to find and seize opportunities. To temper my eagerness and ambition for success, before embarking on an opportunity, I would often ask myself, "Would I be willing to sign my name to this?" In other words, was I willing to be responsible for everything, good or bad, that accompanied the choice to pursue this opportunity? Asking that question determined whether I seized the opportunity or chose to pursue a different course of action.

Today, after asking myself that question thousands of times for more than fifty years, here is what I know:

- The size of the opportunity determines the amount of responsibility required.
- Opportunity is lost when responsibility is neglected.
- Tomorrow's opportunity is determined by yesterday's responsibility.

One of the reasons successful people are successful is that they see and seize a succession of opportunities, taking responsibility for each one. Often we see them going through doors of opportunity, making the most of them, and we think to ourselves, *I wish I had that chance*. We see the results, but what we often don't see is the deep level of personal responsibility they had to take to make the most of each opportunity. Without increasing their responsibility potential, they could not have increased their opportunity potential.

2. Responsibility Puts You in Control of Your Life

The way you take control of the direction of your life is to take responsibility for yourself and your everyday actions. People who embrace responsibility and take control of their lives see dramatic results. Can you control everything? No, of course not. But you can choose to control the things that *are* within your control. First, acknowledge that you have the ability to choose. Then, identify which parts of your life you can control and which you can't. Once you begin taking charge and making choices, your life will begin to change.

If you've ever had the desire to escape from your life, taking responsibility and starting to shape your life will remove much of the temptation to do that. When you give yourself permission to live the life you want, you begin to own yourself and no longer need others' permission to do what you know is right for you. It is at that point that you begin to maximize your capacity.

So take control of what you can control, and don't try to control what you can't control.

3. Responsibility Builds Your Self-Esteem

People often have self-esteem problems because they don't take responsibility for their lives. They blame someone else for the bad things that happen, and then they start to adopt a victim mentality. That never leads to success—or to greater capacity.

When you are faced with a difficult choice to do what you know is right, yet you still do it, how does that make you feel? Doesn't it give you a sense of inner satisfaction? Doesn't it make you feel strong? Doesn't it reward you internally with the sense that you did the right thing? I know it does these things for me. Repeated choices to take responsibility give you mental and emotional momentum, which only makes you feel stronger and better about yourself.

4. Responsibility Makes You Ready for Action

Taking responsibility helps us to become self-starters, and self-starters do very well in life. Why? Because the fastest person is not always the one who wins the race. Often it's the one who started first. Responsible people don't wait around for someone else to take action—*they* do.

Whenever I am faced with a problem, I focus my mind on the issue and remind myself that I am responsible to act. If I lack responsibility, when life calls for action, my response will be ready, aim, aim, aim… but never *fire*. Accepting responsibility makes you take action, not just prepare for it.

5. Responsibility Makes Your Habits Serve You

Are habits good or bad? That, of course, depends on what the habits are and what they do for—or against—us. When we apply responsibility to our habits, it directs them positively and makes them work for us.

Positive habits are decisions that we make once (like deciding to exercise regularly) and then take responsibility for managing daily. When we make a good decision and then manage that decision day to day, we can see positive results through the development of that positive habit. Without management, a good decision dies. With management, the decision lives on. That's why decision-managing is at least as important as decision-making.

Conversely, when we don't take responsibility and neglect to manage our positive habits daily, we often cultivate the negative habits of procrastination, feeling entitled, and making excuses. Before long, those bad habits become our masters. The habit of making excuses creates reasons in our minds for our not being responsible for our lives. Every time we make an excuse, we fail to learn from our mistakes. Excuses put the blame on others or on circumstances, which causes you to give up the power to change your life.

Another negative habit is feeling entitled, believing that whether we win or lose, we deserve a trophy; that whether we work or play, we deserve an income; that whether we do good works or act selfishly, we deserve praise. In essence, when we feel entitled, we want someone else to sponsor us in life without our making any effort of our own. Again, this bad habit masters us and distances us from responsibility.

Recently I was privileged to spend some time with Lou Holtz, a good leader, fantastic football coach, and very funny guy. He said, "The man who complains about the way the ball bounces is likely the one who dropped it." It's OK to drop the ball once in a while. We all do. It's not OK to drop it, blame somebody else, and expect them to pick it up!

Our first responsibility in developing good habits that serve us is to stop the losses (caused by negative habits) that threaten to define us, and start making and managing choices that declare who we are. That all begins when we choose to be responsible, which gives us the power to master our habits—and our lives.

6. Responsibility Earns You Respect and Authority

Respect is gained on difficult ground, and it is not given or granted to us if it is unearned. Often I hear leaders lament their lack of authority. The problem? They rely on titles instead of earning authority through responsible behavior.

Too often we hope for respect instead of earning it the hard way. We avoid the difficult conversation we need to have and hope our problems will just go away. That doesn't happen.

As a young leader who wanted to make people happy, I often told others what they wanted to hear, not what they needed to hear. I didn't take responsibility for speaking the hard truths that good leaders take responsibility for. Today, I welcome responsibility and work to earn the respect of others every day.

Eric Greitens, in his book *Resilience*, describes the bottom line on responsibility. He says, "The more responsibility people take, the more resilient they are likely to be. The less responsibility people take—for their actions, for their lives, for their happiness—the more likely it is that life will crush them. At the root of resilience is the willingness to take responsibility for results." That willingness is also at the root of your potential.

Responsibility Potential Questions

1. In the past, have you ever connected the ideas of taking responsibility and increasing your potential? How, specifically, do you think becoming more responsible could help you in your personal life and career?

2. On a scale of one to ten, how would you rate yourself when it comes to being ready to take action? How might taking greater responsibility increase your readiness?

3. What positive habits would you like to cultivate that could be facilitated by taking greater responsibility? What decision must you make to start the habit, and what actions must you take daily to manage that decision?

9

Character Potential—Your Choices Based on Good Values

At nearly seventy years old, I'm finding that my values are probably deeper and stronger than they have ever been in my life. I rely less and less on beliefs, which I seem to have fewer of as I age. What's the difference? Values don't change, but beliefs do—all the time. Every time you learn something new, your beliefs adjust. In my lifetime I've let go of dozens and dozens of beliefs that I once possessed just because I learned more or experienced more.

Today I am far less interested in certainty about many things and much more interested in clarity about the few things that matter. And though I am certain about fewer things, I have more clarity than I have ever had before in my life. The things that are crystal clear are my values.

Why do I put so much emphasis on values? Because values create the foundation of character, and character provides the foundation for success.

The idea of building character isn't flashy or exciting. It's not something we regularly add to our list of annual goals. But the results of developing character are life changing. It's one of only two or three things I can think of that are *most* important in life.

Here's why character is so important, and why you should make the choices needed to develop your character capacity:

1. Good Character Is a Choice You Can Make Every Day

Every day you either grow your good character or shrink it. When you choose to do the right thing based on a positive value, your character expands. With each right choice, you develop the strength to make other right choices, and more-difficult right choices. In contrast, every time you choose to cut corners, compromise on your values, or turn your back on what you know to be right, it shrinks your character. The smaller and weaker it gets, the more difficult it is to make another right choice.

What are you focused on day to day? Making your work more lucrative? Making your company bigger? Rising up in your organization? Or making your character better, deeper, stronger? The choices you make every day make you.

2. Good Character Speaks Louder Than Words

For several years, I had the privilege of being mentored by legendary UCLA basketball coach John Wooden. He once said, "Be more concerned with your character than your reputation, because your character is what you really are, while your reputation is merely what others think you are."

Who we are inside is much more important than how others see us. Character represents who you really are on the inside: the moral and mental qualities that make you, you. And that is what speaks to people. It speaks more loudly than your words or the words others say about you. Your character represents you to the world.

3. Good Character Is Consistent in All Areas of Life

When a person has good character, he or she has it in every area of life consistently, regardless of circumstances, regardless of setting, and regardless of context. There's no such thing as business ethics—there's only ethics. People try to use one set of ethics for their professional life, another for their spiritual life, and still another at home with their family. That gets them into trouble. Ethics are ethics. If you desire to be ethical, you live by one standard across the board.

Good character uses the same standard in every situation. If something is right, it's always right. If it's wrong, it's always wrong. People with good character are consistent. People who try to use multiple standards with different people and in different situations live fragmented lives.

4. Good Character Engenders Trust

When a person lives a fragmented life, others never know what to expect from him or her. They don't know how the person will act in any given situation. In contrast, a person of good character who lives by the same consistent standard invites trust. People know what they're going to get. They know the person's words and actions will line up. They can rely on that person and what he or she says.

Whenever you make a commitment to another person, you create hope. When you *keep* that commitment, you create trust. Good character helps you to follow through on that commitment and develop that trust. Why is that important? As mentioned in the chapter on people potential, all relationships are built on trust. So by increasing character potential, you build the trust needed to increase people potential. That not only improves the quality of your life but also improves the qualities of your professional relationships, including your ability as a leader. Where trust is absent, leadership falters.

5. Good Character Is Tested in Times of Trouble

Adversity doesn't build character; it reveals it. When you have good character, difficulty only makes you more determined. When your character is weak, difficulty makes you discouraged. Work on your character now. When the storm comes, it's too late to prepare.

6. Good Character Always Takes the High Road

Most people want to treat others the way they've been treated. It's human nature. I once heard a well-known businessman say, "When somebody screws you, screw them back in spades" and "Go for the jugular so that people watching will not want to mess with you." That's not the way I want to live. I don't want to treat others worse than they treat me. I want to treat others better than they treat me. I want to always take the high road.

I hope you'll take a similar path. It's true that sometimes you will be hurt. You will be treated unfairly. People will take advantage of you. But wouldn't you rather make the world a better place and help other people?

7. Good Character Delivers on Its Promises

When you say you'll do something, do you follow through? Are you known as someone who delivers? Or do others sometimes worry that you may give up or not show up? Booker T. Washington said, "Character is power." Make the most of it.

Scientist Marie Curie observed, "You cannot hope to build a better world without improving the individuals. To that end, each of us must work for his own improvement, and at the same time share a general responsibility for all humanity." If you want to build your character, you need to try to align four things: your values, your thinking, your feelings, and your actions. If your values are good and you make the other three things consistent with them, there's almost nothing you can't improve in your life.

Are you willing to do the mundane work of increasing your character capacity? It probably won't receive any fanfare. In fact, you may be the only person who'll ever know what steps you've taken to grow in this area. But I guarantee that you will see positive results and live a better life.

Character Potential Questions

1. Have you ever identified and defined your values and put them into writing? If not, do so now. If so, review them and determine whether they have changed or remain the same?

2. On a scale of 1 to 10, how would you rate yourself on consistency when it comes to acting on your values

through character choices? If you didn't give yourself a 10 (and who does?), what should you start doing differently to raise your score?

3.   When dealing with others, do you most often take the low road, the middle road, or the high road? Why do you respond the way you do? What can you do to become more of a high-road person?

10

Abundance Potential—Your Choice to Believe There Is More Than Enough

How you think in this area determines your choices. That's why you need to focus on changing your thinking about whether or not there's enough to go around. Abundance thinking encourages you to make choices that will expand your possibilities. Scarcity thinking causes you to make choices that will diminish your potential. Abundance calls out to you, "There's more than enough." Scarcity cautions, "Quick, get what you can before it runs out." Abundance says, "Go and you will find the resources." Scarcity says, "Hold on to what you have, because there are no more resources." Abundance says, "Your best days are before you." Scarcity says, "This is as good as it gets." How we act is determined by the voice we allow to speak to us in our minds.

In general, scarcity lives on the other side of "no," meaning people stay where it's safe, while abundance lives on the other side of "yes," meaning they'll try something new. ***What does it look like to live on the other side of no?***

- **It's limiting**—because it directs you away from new opportunities.
- **It's easy**—because when you say no, you don't have to do anything or go anywhere.
- **It's comforting**—because it feels familiar. Many people are more fearful of losing the little they do have than they are excited about gaining something they don't have.
- **It's deceiving**—because it appears to be safer, but it's not.
- **It's crowded**—because it's where average people live.

What does it look like to live on the other side of yes?

- **It's exciting**—because you need creativity to help you figure things out when they're new.
- **It's enlarging**—because abundance creates more abundance. And the more abundance you experience, the greater your potential.
- **It's challenging**—because new paths are not easy to tread.

- **It's rewarding**—because on the other side of yes, you usually find many more yeses.

I realize that no is not always bad and yes is not always good, but most of the time, living a life of no decreases your options, opportunities, and outcomes, while living on the other side of yes increases you and your world.

People with high abundance potential believe the answer is yes. There is a way to move forward. It may not be easy to find, it may not be the first choice, but they believe there is a way. And that's how I want you to think. I want to help you adopt an abundance mind-set and increase your capacity in this area. Even if you're a bit of a skeptic, I hope you are willing to give it a try. I hope you'll take a look at these three ways people of abundance think and make the choice to embrace them:

1. Abundance People Possess High Belief

Why are people who embrace abundance able to say yes so readily? It's because they possess high belief in many areas of life:

THEY BELIEVE IN THEMSELVES—THEY SAY, "THERE'S MORE TO ME THAN WHAT PEOPLE SEE"

Beliefs drive behavior. Lack of belief, which is a characteristic of scarcity, holds us back. We hesitate, not because we are unable to do something but because we don't have confidence in ourselves. My friend, don't wait for someone else to pick you. Don't wait for someone to give you permission. You don't need anyone else to say you are qualified. Believe in yourself! Believe you can.

THEY BELIEVE IN OTHERS—THEY SAY, "THERE'S MORE TO OTHERS THAN I CAN SEE"

When people believe in each other, they want the best for each other and expect the best from each other. They bless one another. Professor and author Dallas Willard defines *blessing* this way: "the projection of good toward someone." I love that. I want to live that. Don't you?

THEY BELIEVE IN TODAY—THEY SAY, "THERE'S MORE IN TODAY THAN I CAN SEE"

Abundance people seize the moment because they see potential in it. They believe they can do more than they've done before. They believe they can perform at a higher level than they have before. They believe they can grow more—and keep growing. This belief not only keeps them going but also allows them to be the first to take action. And often those who start first are the winners.

THEY BELIEVE IN TOMORROW—THEY SAY, "THERE'S MORE IN MY FUTURE THAN I CAN SEE"

Have you noticed how old people think their generation is the last great one? They look at younger people and predict doom and gloom. That's happened for a hundred generations. I'm not going to do that! Yes, tomorrow has its challenges. And all youths need to mature. But abundance thinking tells us that tomorrow can be better than today. It charges us up with high belief. That high belief gives us high energy. I want to be energized to do worthwhile things and make a difference. Don't you?

2. Abundance People Understand the Power of Perspective

Our perspective is not determined by what we see. It's determined by *how* we see, and that comes from who we are. Two people can be in the same situation and see things completely differently. While a scarcity person often looks at a situation and thinks, *There's no way!* an abundance person sees the same thing and thinks, *There's got to be a better way!* The world is a better place as a result of people whose perspective was shaped by abundance thinking. Change your perspective to one of abundance from one of scarcity, and you open the door to innovation and positive change, not only for yourself but also for others.

3. Abundance People Are Generous to Others

When most people think of generosity, they usually think about giving money to charity. While that is truly a mark of generosity, there are other kinds of generosity that have nothing to do with money. These include giving people a chance, giving others the benefit of the doubt, and giving others a reason to want to work with you. An abundance person can be generous by giving others opportunities, giving them the resources and information they need to do their jobs well, giving them the credit when they are successful, and giving them grace when they make mistakes. What I'm really talking about here is generosity of spirit.

If you're a leader, you need to understand that by virtue of your position and the privileges it brings, you should be generous toward the people you lead. I wish all leaders held themselves to this high standard, though not all do. The leaders who bring an abundance mind-set to their leadership responsibilities can increase the positive impact they make on their teams and organizations.

Some people worry that if they give too much of what they have, they will run short themselves. But I would say the opposite is true. The more you give, the more you get. And that just helps you to become more generous. You can see this in action when you smile at others. What happens when you do that? You usually receive a smile back. And that just makes you want to smile more. The more you help other people, the more they usually want to help others. And that motivates you to help even more. That's what I call the Abundance Paradox. The more you give, the more you have to give—and want to give.

I believe you can step out of the scarcity world and become an abundance person, even if you grew up feeling like there's not enough. Why do I say that? Because I've seen people who started out with a scarcity mindset choose to become people of abundance.

Abundance people don't run out by giving. The opposite is true. They sow into the lives of others and receive a great harvest as a result. Without question, my greatest return on investment in life has been believing in and investing in other people. Generous people are always interested in increasing the lives of those around them. And people will always move toward anyone who increases them and away from anyone who makes them feel like less.

If you're like most people, in your heart you'd like to believe in abundance. My advice to you is follow your heart. It was created for abundance. Talk to yourself. Say aloud, "I believe there is more than enough." That's a small step in the right direction, toward abundance. And sometimes the smallest step in the right direction becomes the biggest step in your life.

Abundance Potential Questions

1. When faced with an opportunity, are you naturally a yes person or a no person? If abundance usually means saying yes, what can you do to prompt yourself to say yes more often?

2. Belief in abundance begins with a person's belief in him- or herself. How would you rate your self-belief? Is it high, medium, or low? What must you do to raise it and put yourself in a position to embrace a stronger abundance mind-set?

3. What are you currently looking at in your life and saying, "There's no way"? Pick something important to you. Tell yourself, "There's got to be a better way." Then start brainstorming ideas for how you can move forward positively.

11

Discipline Potential—Your Choice to Focus Now and Follow Through

Successful people are highly disciplined in doing their most important work. They are self-disciplined. They guide and encourage themselves to do the work they ought to do, not just the things they want to do. That's what takes them from average to good, and from good to great. And that's why the rewards in this world are usually reserved for those who are willing to do what the majority of people are unwilling to do.

Success does not come looking for us. We won't achieve great things accidentally. Never forget: everything worthwhile is uphill. Achieving what you want takes time, effort, consistency, energy, and commitment. Self-discipline is what makes those things possible and puts success within reach. And here's the good news: self-discipline is something you can develop. You don't need to be born with it. It's a choice you make and keep on making.

If you'd like to see your potential for discipline increase, take these ideas to heart and put them into practice.

1. Know What Is Important

Do you know what's important to you? If you haven't thought it through and written it out, it's very likely that any lack of self-discipline you're experiencing is coming from that. The single greatest way to increase your discipline capacity is to know what's important and have that as a touchstone for your life.

2. Get Rid of Excuses

If discipline is the highway that takes us where we want to go in life, then excuses are exits off that highway. And believe me—there are *lots* of exits. Take a look at some of these and see if you've ever found yourself saying any of them:

- I'll start after the new year.
- I don't want to do it alone.
- I'll do it when I have more energy.
- I'll do it when I'm not as busy.
- I'll do it when I retire.

- I'm too inexperienced.
- I'm too afraid.
- I don't know how to start.

I've used a few of those myself, but I'm not proud of it.

How do you know something is an excuse? Ask yourself, "Would it stop me from doing something I love to do?" If it wouldn't, it's an excuse. Get rid of it.

3. Take Action before You Feel Like It

The message we hear over and over is that we should do what we feel like doing. But what if we don't feel like doing something? Should we wait for inspiration? In the case of writing, every experienced writer will tell you that you have to write when you don't feel like it. Otherwise, you'll never get much done.

Every person has a weak area that is especially hard to discipline. So how can you make yourself take action before you feel like it? Here are three places to start that work for me:

- Think about the consequences of not acting.
- Focus on doing the right thing just for today.
- Make yourself accountable to someone else in your weak area.

What systems do you have in place to prompt you to take the right action when you don't feel like it? Who have you enlisted to hold you accountable? No matter how much self-discipline you have, you could benefit from ways to help you take action when it counts.

4. Don't Let Distractions Distract You

Brian Tracy observed, "Successful men and women are those who work almost all the time on high value tasks. Unsuccessful men and women are those who waste their time by wasting the minutes and hours of each day on low value activities."

He calls this the Crowding Out Principle. It goes like this: "If you spend all of your time on highly productive tasks, by the end of the day, you will have 'crowded out' all the unproductive activities that might have distracted you from your real work. On the other hand, if you spend your time on low value activities, those low value activities will crowd out the time that you need to complete the tasks that can make all the difference in your life. And the key to this attitude toward time and personal management is always self-discipline."[2]

Ask yourself, "What am I crowding out of my life these days?" Are you doing the unimportant or the convenient at the expense of the essential? I hope not, because if you are, you're going to be in trouble. You aren't expending your energy on what really matters.

5. Be Aware of Time

I have never known a person who lacked awareness of time who was self-disciplined. Successful people are time conscious; they know how they spend the time they have, and they understand that every minute matters.

If you want to maximize the time you have, then I recommend that you do these two things that I do continually:

SET EXPECTATIONS UP FRONT

Have you ever noticed that the completion of tasks often fills whatever time we allot to it? If you give yourself a day, it takes a day. If you say to yourself, "I have to get this done in two hours," it will take the entire two hours.

Start setting expectations for yourself and others up front. Once you make this a regular practice, you can begin compressing the time you allot and keep compressing it until you figure out how efficient you truly can be with your time. Then you'll know how quickly you can get things done and set aggressive yet realistic time frames for meetings and tasks.

SET EXTERNAL DEADLINES

So much of what we do in life has no deadline. As a result, many things get put off and float from day to day on our to-do lists. That's why I give myself external deadlines for nearly everything I want to get done.

Every week, I look at my schedule, determine what I need to get done, and give myself deadlines. Every day I keep these deadlines on a piece of paper on my desk where I can always see it. These visible deadlines create an awareness of time for me. They keep me moving mentally.

Expectations and deadlines are great friends for any disciplined person. Try using them. I believe you will be amazed at how they increase your discipline capacity and your use of time.

6. Follow Through, Even When It Hurts

To be successful, we need to do what we should, even when it hurts. Self-discipline is the fuel that keeps you going. The willingness to hold on in spite of problems, the power to endure—this is a winner's quality.

Say to yourself each morning, "Today isn't over until I've finished whatever I need to do this day." Don't finish your day until what you set out to do has been done. Respect yourself enough to keep the promises you make in the morning.

You cannot manage your life if you do not manage yourself. You cannot maximize your potential if you cannot increase your discipline. Life continually gets busier and more complicated. It doesn't go the other way. If you're older, as I am, you recognize that. If I live to be a hundred, it won't be enough time to accomplish all the dreams I have.

I can't have any more hours in a day. So what can I do? Two things. First, I can expand my discipline potential, so that I make the most of the time I *do* have. Second, I can partner with others (which I'll talk about in chapter 17). To increase your discipline, you don't have to be rich. You don't have to be a genius. You don't need to come from a great family. You don't need extraordinary talent. You just need to focus and follow through.

Discipline Potential Questions

1. Self-discipline is where time and priorities meet. What would happen if you looked at your schedule and to-do list every week and allotted specific amounts of time for everything? How much time would that take? And how much time would that save you?

2. What excuses have become a normal part of your life? Write a list of the ones you often find yourself using, and then write the counterargument to each so that you can be more self-disciplined in the future.

3. What percentage of the time do you follow through? The times when you don't, when do you stop and why? Is there a pattern? What can you do to push through at those times?

12

Intentionality Potential—Your Choice to Deliberately Pursue Significance

The greatest way for you to upgrade your life is to become intentional with it. When people increase their capacity for intentionality, everything else changes in their lives. When you become more intentional, your life can transform from successful to significant.

Significance is all about adding value to others. That's an uphill journey. Why? Because we are naturally selfish. We automatically think of ourselves first. If you don't believe that, let me ask you a question. When someone takes a photo of a group that you're in and then shows it to you, who is the first person you look for? Case dismissed! You look for yourself. That's not an accusation. I look for myself, too. It's proof that we're all selfish. Selfishness is a downhill habit. Significance is an uphill trait. But it is achievable for you and for me.

I want to teach you my five daily essentials for adding value to people. If you do these things every day, you will make a difference and you will immediately feel the significance of your life.

1. Every Day, Value People

People don't add value to others when they don't value others. So why should you value others? Because they're people. You don't need any other reason. Listen, human beings are human. They make mistakes. They say the wrong things. They hurt our feelings. Many people treat us poorly and are not very lovable. Love them anyway.

You know how you feel when others devalue you and how you feel when they value you. Doesn't it make a difference to you? How you're treated impacts how you feel about yourself and how you treat others. Keep that in mind as you interact with people. When you value others, you start creating a cycle of positive interaction that makes life better for everyone.

2. Every Day, Think of Ways to Add Value to People

If I said I had a five-minute thinking exercise for you that would give you a huge return in your relationships, would you be interested? Of course you would. Here's what I want you to do. Spend five minutes every evening thinking about who you will see the next day, and ask yourself, "What can I say to them, give to them, or do for them that will make our time together memorable, be unexpected, and add value to them?"

That sounds too simple, doesn't it? But trust me, this exercise will set you apart from 99 percent of all the other people in the world. And if you do this every evening and then revisit the ideas you come up with the next morning to potentially improve them, you will be amazed by the difference you can make for other people.

People who make a difference think about ways to add value to people ahead of time. Take a look at your day's calendar. Where will you be going? Who will you be meeting? In what ways might you add value to someone else? It only takes five minutes, but the opportunities to make a difference are endless.

3. Every Day, Look for Ways to Add Value to People

If the previous tip was about planning ways to add value before the day starts, this one is about going through every moment of your day on the lookout for additional ways to add value to others. It's proactive and ongoing.

Since I spend so much time speaking and writing, I'm always looking for ideas and information I can use to help me help others. It has become part of my mindset. And when I do find something useful to pass on, I ask myself, "Where can I use this? When can I use this? Who needs to know this?"

As you go through your day, what is your mind-set? Are you intentionally looking for ways to add value to others? If not, you can. It's a capacity choice. If you choose to look for ways, you'll find them.

4. Every Day, Do Things That Add Value to People

It's not enough to just look for ways to help people. You have to follow through if you want to make a difference. Intentional living requires intentional doing.

How do I know I've had a good day? When I say yes to the question I ask myself every night, "Did I add value to someone today?" My ultimate goal in adding value to others is to do something for them that they cannot do for themselves.

Mother Teresa said, "Let no one ever come to you without leaving better and happier. Be a living expression of God's kindness: kindness in your face, kindness in your eyes, kindness in your smile, kindness in your warm greeting." That's something all of us can strive for.

5. Every Day, Encourage Others to Add Value to People

I believe nothing is as common as the desire to make our lives count, to make a difference. And there are needs all around us waiting to be met by intentional people. Yet so many never live a significant life. Why? Because doing the right thing is more difficult than knowing the right thing. That's why we need to encourage others to act.

As you make the choice to add value to others and develop the first four habits I outlined in the chapter, don't forget the fifth and final step of encouraging others to do the same. You'll be amazed at what can happen when like-minded and like-valued people work together to add value to others and make a difference.

You can be someone who makes a difference. You just need to try to help someone every day. That's what intentional living is. Every time you think about ways to help others and take action, you're increasing your intentionality potential, making a difference, and achieving significance with your life.

Intentionality Potential Questions

1. How do you most enjoy adding value to people? What could you do that you would enjoy but haven't done yet? When can you start doing it?

2. How will you add value to people in the next twenty-four hours? Try anticipating ways you could

add value to people on your schedule. You should also look for opportunities in the moment as you go through your day.

3.   Whom could you encourage to add value to people? What could you do to encourage them?

13

Attitude Potential—Your Choice to Be Positive Regardless of Circumstances

No single change you make in your life will have a greater positive impact on you and those around you than making a choice to improve your attitude. If your attitude isn't as good as you would like it to be, start the process of improving it by recognizing these truths. You may want to say them aloud:

1. **"I need to change."** Change is personal. Only you can do it for yourself.
2. **"I'm able to change."** Change is possible. Many others have changed.
3. **"I'll be rewarded for change."** Change is profitable. You will see results.

Your attitude is one of the most pliable and resilient parts of you. Regardless of your age or circumstances, you can change it if you're willing to.

When I am in need of an attitude adjustment, I practice self-talk. In fact, what I really do is coach myself on my attitude continually throughout the day. Why? Because it's so easy to become discouraged without a good attitude. The greatest separator between successful and unsuccessful people is how they deal with and explain their failures, problems, and difficulties.

When something happens *to* you, recognize that it is external. Identify the source of the problem and say to yourself, "This happened because of that." Remind yourself that it is changeable. You're not trapped. Tell yourself, "I can make changes to prevent this from happening again." And finally, know that just because something negative happened, it won't be that way forever. Tell yourself, "It was a solitary occurrence. It doesn't have to affect the rest of my life."

Positive self-talk is one of the most important tools I have to keep my attitude positive. When something goes wrong, I say something like this: "Wow! That didn't go the way I expected. OK. That's not what I wanted, but I can get through this. I win more often than I lose, but no one goes undefeated. Now, what can I learn from what I just experienced? What do I need to change? Is there someone who can help me? Because of this, I'll become better, but I won't become bitter. This too shall pass."

Coaching and encouraging yourself is huge when it comes to choosing a positive attitude regardless of circumstances. It is the single best thing you can do to help yourself. That being said, there are some foundational things you can do to put yourself in a positive position most of the time. By doing the following things, you make it easier for yourself to bounce back from difficulties.

1. Remain Humble

It is much easier to face life's difficulties and respond positively when you display humility. How do you do that? I love this advice I once heard: "Not all of us can do great things. But we can do small things with great love." Doing small things that may seem unimportant to us but that benefit others helps us cultivate humility. Doing them with love builds on that.

2. Be Teachable

Teachability is an attitude of wanting to learn from every experience and every person. It requires an appreciation for everything we experience, knowing that we can always learn something—if we have the right spirit.

As a young leader, I didn't always display that spirit.

I was not especially teachable. I was more interested in looking good than I was in getting better. I wanted to teach others more than I wanted to be taught. Because I wanted to look good, I covered up my mistakes and didn't look at my failures. As a result, I missed important lessons I could have learned. Those things are not true of me anymore. My passion to learn has done nothing but grow. And it's still growing. Because I want to learn from everyone and everything, it allows me to learn from everyone and everything. That's a teachable spirit.

What is your attitude toward learning—from your mistakes, from your difficult circumstances, from others who want to help you, from others who oppose you? Are you ready to learn? Teachability not only displays a positive attitude, but it also fosters a positive attitude.

3. Become Resilient

To maintain a positive attitude, you need to be resilient and not let anything negative take hold of you. Time spent being angry about the past means less time spent moving forward and doing what you desire to do. I keep very short accounts and don't carry any emotional baggage in my life. Why? Because while I'm holding a grudge against someone and nursing my hurt feelings, they're probably out dancing. If you think someone or something other than yourself is responsible for your success or happiness, then you will be neither happy nor successful. You have to learn how to bounce back from rejection.

Resilient people have a positive outlook. They know that the difficulties they're facing are only temporary. They reflect on the fact that they've overcome problems and setbacks before and survived. And they can do it again. Resilient people don't focus on the negative experience. They focus on what they can learn from the experience.

4. Maintain Perspective

I think it is very easy for us to lose perspective in life and get discouraged. If your attitude is wrong, it's difficult for anything else in your life to be right. Too often we see a single victory as a finish line, or a single loss as a grave. The reality is that life is a long game. If it were a baseball game, there would be thirty thousand innings. (That's one inning a day for more than eighty years.) If it were a race, it would be more than eighty thousand miles. (That's a 5K every day.) If it were—you get the idea. We need to have the right perspective and remain positive because there are still a lot of at bats or miles ahead of us.

Perspective is especially important if you're a leader. As leaders, what we want to do is help the members of our team to cross the finish line with us so we can all celebrate together. Your attitude as a leader sets the tone for the team as they race. It's difficult to start the race, run it with excellence, and make it to the finish line unless we maintain a positive attitude. If you're a leader, you can't afford to ignore the importance of attitude. And if you're not a leader—you can't afford to ignore the importance of attitude.

Years ago I determined that attitude is a choice. Since that time I haven't felt sorry for anyone who chooses to have a bad attitude. I just try to help the ones I can by encouraging them to increase their attitude potential. And as for the ones who won't change, I just try to avoid them.

If your attitude gets better because your circumstances improve, then that says nothing about your attitude. It's only a sign that your situation has changed. How can you tell that your attitude has gotten better? You know that your attitude capacity has increased when your attitude is remaining positive even as your difficulties rise. When that happens, you know you can weather almost any storm and come out of it better than ever.

Attitude Potential Questions

1. What kind of self-talk do you engage in? Have you ever paid attention to it? If not, take some time to observe it. What could you do to make what you say to yourself more positive?

2. How would you score yourself in the areas of humility, teachability, resilience, and perspective? Which of the four could you most readily improve? What can you do immediately to improve it?

3. If there is so much evidence that having a good attitude makes people happier and more productive, why do you believe people still choose to have negative attitudes? What could you do to encourage others to choose to have more positive attitudes?

14

Risk Potential—Your Choice to Get Out of Your Comfort Zone

Not everyone is a natural risk-taker. Perhaps you're facing a risky challenge right now. Or you are considering taking on a high-risk project. Or maybe you desire to do something significant, and you sense that something big but risky is on the horizon. If so, I know how you are feeling, because I've been in your shoes.

On the other hand, maybe you've been risk averse your whole life, and you recognize how much it has held you back and limited your potential. No matter what your circumstances are, here are some things you need to know that will help you to take more risks:

1. Reality Is Your Friend during High-Risk Times

When taking big risks, you can't depend on hype or wishful thinking, because those things cannot withstand the heat of risk. You need to understand what you're dealing with, examine the worst-case scenarios, and look reality dead in the eye.

How do you look reality in the eye when evaluating a risk? Ask yourself some questions:

- Who else has done it?
- How bad can it get?
- How good can it get?
- Can I try it on for size?
- Is there room for error?
- Do I believe in myself?

The more questions you ask and answer, the better prepared you are to weigh the risk and gauge whether the risk is smart or foolish.

2. You Must Learn to Become Comfortable outside of Your Comfort Zone

Risk is rarely comfortable. It requires us to get out of our comfort zone. That's where we need to live when we're risking big. How do you deal with that? For me, anything worthwhile that I've ever done initially scared me to death. First speech? Frightened beyond belief. First board meeting? Scared stiff. I was never good the first time, and I was always scared on top of that.

You have to deal with your emotions and doubts.

To continually succeed in high-risk environments, you have to be continually comfortable being uncomfortable. How? Start with these three strategies:

DON'T LOOK IN THE MIRROR

Take the focus off of yourself; you need to always keep in mind that life is not about you. You can't worry about how you look to others. You can't be afraid of looking bad.

DON'T COUNT LOSSES—INSTEAD, COUNT LESSONS

Instead of avoiding losses, learn from them. Ask, "What did I learn?" When you seek lessons more than you avoid losses, you become more comfortable with risk.

FOCUS LESS ON YOUR FEAR AND MORE ON YOUR DREAMS

When you focus on your dreams, your heart is 100 percent in.

3. Good Leadership Gives You a Greater Chance for Success

Everything rises and falls on leadership. That is never truer than during times of risk. The size of the leadership must be equal to the size of the risk. If you're going to attempt something difficult, you need good leadership. You need to either provide it yourself or find a partner who can help you lead. And if you're going to try something huge, you'll need lots of leaders. Any great attempt without great leadership is destined to fizzle out.

If you are preparing to take a big risk, it may require every leadership skill you possess to accomplish it. Don't take that lightly. Keep growing as a leader. The more you increase your leadership potential, the more you increase your capacity for risk.

And if you're already a leader, you also need to provide others with a pro-risk environment so that they're willing to deal with their fears and take steps forward, outside of their comfort zones.

4. The Bigger the Risk, the More Help You'll Need from Others

While it's fun to dream about the potential upside of any risky venture, the reality of it can make us want to yell "HELP!" at the top of our lungs. The greater and riskier the venture, the greater our need for help. And to be successful, you don't just need help; you need the right kind of help.

Mass movements don't begin with the masses. They always begin with a few. But if those few are the right people, there is the potential for a mass movement. What are the characteristics of the right people?

THEY LIKE A CHALLENGE

When you cast a vision for something big, it is both a uniter and divider. People of high capacity who like a challenge rally to you. Small people leave. The size of the vision determines the size of the person who signs up.

They Play Big

What's more dangerous than playing big? Never taking a risk. When you're doing nothing, nothing good happens. You want people willing to join you in taking a big risk, to try something new, even if it's difficult.

They Are Honest with Themselves

When you're attempting something difficult, you want people on your team who know themselves and are honest with themselves. They have to know what they're capable of and know what the stakes are. And as a leader, you need to help make sure they know those things.

Even if you're not someone who owns a company, holds a leadership position, or leads some kind of team, you may still need help when you tackle a risk. Look for like-minded people who are willing to face challenges to assist you. It will greatly increase your risk capacity.

5. Taking Risks Always Requires Personal Courage

If you want to expand your potential, and therefore your life, you need to be willing to take greater risks. You need to be willing to stand alone. You need to gather the courage to do what others might not do—not just for the sake of doing something bold and risky but because you can see the potential reward.

What's great about taking smart risks is that it not only expands your possibilities, but it also inspires other people to want to join you in your efforts. People follow courage. When someone is willing to stand alone in the beginning and face opposition, they can earn respect and credibility. Eventually, others see their courage and rally around them.

So what are you going to do? Are you willing to increase your risk potential? Are you willing to fail doing something big? Are you willing to count lessons more than losses? Are you willing to model the way by becoming comfortable outside of your comfort zone?

These are not small things. But if you're not willing to do them, you'd better become comfortable with only small things. Because you'll accomplish big things only if you're willing to take big risks. I hope you are.

Risk Potential Questions

1. How good are you at facing reality and assessing the odds when you prepare to take a risk? If you're not especially good at it, who can you enlist to help you count the cost?

2. When you prepare to take a big risk, how much consideration do you normally give to leadership and the formation of a team to help you? Explain. How must you change to improve in this area?

3. Have you learned how to deal with the discomfort of being out of your comfort zone? Have you learned how to function in spite of your fear? Or does being in risky territory stop you? What must you do to grow in this area?

15

Spiritual Potential—Your Choice to Strengthen Your Faith

This is a chapter that I *had* to write. I'm writing about my relationship with God. My faith choice has been instrumental to increasing my potential in every area of my life. My choice to strengthen my faith has done more to enable me to grow than any of the other choices in this book. However, everyone makes his or her own choice in this area. So if this subject bothers you, you can stop reading and skip ahead to chapter 16.

I want your spiritual potential to increase. I want your return to be high on the investment you make in your work. I want your relationships to flourish. I want you to have your greatest years ahead of you. So I'm praying for you. Specifically, here is my prayer for an increase in your spiritual capacity, based on a passage in Ephesians 3:14–20:

1. I Pray That You Will Know God

Ephesians 3:14–17 says, "My response is to get down on my knees before the Father, this magnificent Father who parcels out all heaven and earth. I ask him to strengthen you by his Spirit—not a brute strength but a glorious inner strength—that Christ will live in you as you open the door and invite him in."[3]

It's amazing and humbling to me that Christ wants to live in me. I know me, and sometimes I don't even want to live with myself. But God does. What a beautiful picture of God that paints. If you are 1,000 steps from God, He will take 999 steps in your direction. And then He will wait for you to open your heart and ask Him into your life. God wants you to want a relationship with Him.

2. I Pray That You Will Experience God's Love

The passage in Ephesians continues: "And I ask him that with both feet planted firmly on love, you'll be able to take in with all Christians the extravagant dimensions of Christ's love. Reach out and experience the breadth! Test its length! Plumb the depths! Rise to the heights! Live full lives, full in the fullness of God."[4]

God wants us to live a full life with full capacity. He truly wants the best for us. Jesus said, "I have come that they might have life, and have it abundantly!"[5] As you read that statement, did you notice the comma? Which side of the comma do you live on? Are you living the life of abundance you desire? That's what Jesus offers. He offers extravagant love and life at its fullest. The most wonderful joy is to have a relationship with God and experience His amazing love.

When Scripture says that God's love has breadth, it means that God's love includes everyone—of every faith, of every race, of every nationality, and of every age or stage of life.

God asks us to test the length of His love. What is its length? Forever! God's love is never-ending. And the best part of that is that His love doesn't depend on me or on you. God loves you as you are, not as you would like to be, or as you appear to be, but just as you are. And nothing you can do can make Him love you more!

What does it mean to plumb God's depths? The implication is that no matter how low you go, God's love is deeper. God is forgiving. For many of us, the bad news is that our capacity to sin has taken us lower than we ever believed we would go. The good news is that God's capacity to forgive us is greater. In fact, God not only forgives our sins, but He also forgets our sins. He said, "I will be merciful to them in their wrongdoings, and I will remember their sins no more."[6] Wow!

Rising to the height of God's love means being lifted up by Him. There is no one more uplifting than God. God wants you to reach your full potential. He created you with a plan and gave you gifts to help you accomplish that plan. He will be the greatest lifter in your life if you let Him.

3. I Pray That You Will Allow God to Do Great Things in Your Life

As you read the rest of the passage from Ephesians, embrace the words, because they are for you: "God can do anything, you know—far more than you could ever imagine or guess or request in your wildest dreams! He does it not by pushing us around but by working within us, his Spirit deeply and gently within us."[7]

These words apply to you, but they must be activated by your faith. Jesus said, "According to your faith will it be done to you."[8] I call this the faith factor. There are many factors that influence your life over which you have no control: your background, nationality, age, giftedness. These were determined by the sovereignty of God. But there is one important factor you do have control over: how much you choose to believe God. God puts no limitation on faith; faith puts no limitation on God.

Every year in December, I pray and ask God to give me a word or phrase for the coming year. In 2016, I sensed that my phrase for the year was "God Room." Today, those are the words I use to express my faith. What do I mean by "God Room"? Let me explain by quoting again from the above statements in Ephesians:

GOD ROOM IS ALL ABOUT GOD

God can do anything.

These words should set the bar of our expectations about God at a very high level. We need to be aware of how great a space there is between what we can do and what He can do. That's God Room—room for God to do what only He can do. We do the possible. God does the impossible. That shows us who He is.

GOD ROOM IS BIGGER THAN I AM

God can do anything, you know—far more than you could ever imagine or guess or request in your wildest dreams!

How much is far more? It's not a *little* more or *some* more. It's *far* more. It's so much more that I don't think we can comprehend it. Don't even try to understand how much bigger God is than us. We can't. No words can ever come close. God is God and we are not. That is both simple and humbling. If we can explain our life and believe we can solve everything in it, then we're not giving God room to live in it.

GOD ROOM IS A PLACE WITHIN ME WHERE I CHOOSE TO LET GOD DO WHAT ONLY HE CAN DO

He does it not by pushing us around but by working within us, his Spirit deeply and gently within us.

God doesn't force anything on us, not even His love.

He offers it to us gently. And He works within us only because we choose to let Him do that. Now that is a huge potential choice. The question we all have to answer is simply, "How much room will we give God?" It's like His love; we can experience as much as we desire.

GOD ROOM IS UNEXPLAINABLE AND UNDENIABLE

Perhaps the most amazing thing about God Room is that God allows average people like you and me to have access to it. And as a result, God can do amazing things with and through us. We don't have much to offer God except ourselves. God wants our willingness, not our strengths. If you think you can do everything on your own and you're searching for some secret reservoir of strength, then stop. Because there isn't one. Focus on God's endless resources. He can do what we cannot do. And He's willing to do it if you're willing to give Him credit for it.

That's my prayer for you. And I will continue to pray for you.

I'm glad you decided to read this chapter. God's invitation is extended to you. He loves you. I hope you will accept that love, if you haven't already. Not only will it maximize your potential, but it also will change every aspect of your life. If you don't yet know God, you have no idea what He can and will do for you.

Spiritual Potential Questions

1. Up until now, how did you think of God? Is what you read in this chapter consistent with your beliefs, or did you learn something new?

2. When you read that God loves you no matter what and that you can do nothing to make Him love you more than He already does, how did that make you feel?

3. What action do you intend to take in response to God's invitation to you?

16

Growth Potential—Your Choice to Focus on How Far You Can Go

In this chapter, I want to share with you what a growth environment looks like. If you possess a fixed mind-set, then putting yourself in a growth environment will help you to change, grow, and adapt. If you already have a growth mind-set, then a growth environment will accelerate your development and increase your capacity at a higher rate. And if you happen to be a leader, you can study the characteristics of a growth environment and begin to *create* one within your department or organization that will help develop your team members.

I've studied different environments and created a few as a leader. In my forty-plus years of experience, I've identified ten characteristics of a positive growth environment:

1. Others Are Ahead of You

Are you at the head of your class? If so, then you're in the wrong class. You need to find people who are ahead of you so that you can learn from them. All my life I have been very intentional about finding people who are faster, better, smarter, bigger, and older than I am to learn from. I always stretch better when someone is ahead of me. So will you.

In your environment, are there people who are ahead of you? If not, you need to find some.

2. You Are Continually Challenged

Some of the most significant things in life take great time and effort. The joy of the journey toward them comes from the new discoveries we make along the way. Our new knowledge and discoveries become the motivation for us to continue the journey. It is only after we go a long distance that we can look back and realize what we didn't know. Soon we begin to realize that it is not the destination that we're seeking. Rather, we desire the growth that we experience, and we find ourselves embracing the journey with full knowledge that there is no finish line. At that time, we stop asking, "How long will it take?" and begin to wonder, *How far can I go?*

3. Your Focus Is Forward

In a positive growth environment, your focus is on moving forward. Old people talk a lot about yesterday. They reminisce about the "good ole days." Well, let me tell you, the good ole days weren't that good. Old people just think they were because they're old and can't remember. I don't want to look back. And neither should you.

4. The Atmosphere Is Affirming

People do best when they are encouraged. Do you live and work in an environment where you are affirmed for being who you are? Do people encourage you to grow and cheer you on when you make choices that make you better? If so, you know how much that helps. If not, you need to find a place where people build each other up, not pull them down.

5. You Are out of Your Comfort Zone

You've read an entire chapter on risk and getting out of your comfort zone, so I don't need to say too much here. But I do want to tell you this: there is no growth in your comfort zone and no comfort in your growth zone. So are you getting out of your comfort zone on a regular basis?

6. You Wake Up Excited

One of the great mysteries in life to me is the number of bored people in this world. They yawn when they wake up and keep yawning all day. I can't live that way. Every day I wake up with a feeling of excitement. Do you wake up excited every morning? Every day we have a choice to explore and make the most of our opportunities for growth or ignore them. What choice are you making?

7. Failure Is Not Your Enemy

In a growth environment you are allowed—or even encouraged—to fail. You know that failure is not your enemy when...

- You value the lessons failure has taught you.
- It helps you to develop resilience.
- You use your failures to teach others.

Failure is inevitable; learning is optional. I've found that my passion for trying is greater than my fear of failing. You'll know you have lost your fear of failure when you are not afraid to share those failures with other people.

8. Others Are Growing

If you do not see other people around you growing, then you know you're not in a growth environment. If you want to grow into your goals, you'll benefit greatly from being surrounded by others who are growing.

Not everyone wants to grow. After several failed attempts to help others develop, I started asking the people

I would like to develop to answer three questions—before I would start helping them:

> *Do* you want to grow?
> *Will* you do it?
> *Can* you do it?

The answers need to be yes, or else why waste the time and effort trying to invest in them? Their answers determine my effort.

9. People Desire Change

There are many doors of opportunity that lie before you. You must open and walk through those doors in order to go to the next level of your life. Many of those doors will not be what they seemed in the beginning. There will be times when you'll need to turn around, close that door, and go in a different direction. That's OK. This is all a part of change. When a door doesn't lead somewhere worthwhile, make a U-turn. As you explore new opportunities, keep these ideas in mind:

- Don't be afraid of backtracking. When you do it correctly, you haven't lost ground; you've just found your footing.
- Don't close a door until you know the lesson you have learned from that experience.

- Don't close a door to quit. Go to another door. When you leave something, have something to go to.
- If you keep opening and closing the same doors, the problem is not lack of opportunities. The problem is you. Ask the people who know you best and love you most to speak honestly into your life.

Change can be difficult to master, yet change is always required for growth. I hope you find these insights about doors of opportunity helpful as you navigate through uncharted waters.

10. Growth Is Modeled and Expected

In my book *The 15 Invaluable Laws of Growth*, I teach the Law of Modeling, which says it's hard to improve when you have no one but yourself to follow. That's why good modeling and an expectation of growth are so important in a positive growth environment. Ideally, that modeling should occur from the very top all the way down into every area of the organization. Nobody is too high or too low to grow.

You can determine if you're in an environment where growth is modeled and expected by asking these two questions:

- Who brings the best out of me in this organization?
- Who do I bring the best out of in this organization?

If you can readily list the names of people who are bringing the best out in you and others could write your name as a model of growth, then you are in a growth environment.

I hope you will make growth a priority for yourself and the people in your life today. It is one of the most important and profitable choices you can make. It's like building your own vehicle, getting out on the open road, and choosing your own destination. It's being as active as you can be in your own destiny.

Growth Potential Questions

1. How many of the ten characteristics described in the chapter does your current environment possess? What does that say about that environment? Do you need to make any changes? If so, what are they?

2. Whom have you actively chosen to mentor you in your life? Do you currently have a mentor? If not, whom should you approach to help you become better?

3. What direction would you like to go in your life? How do you need to grow to get there? What steps can you take today to start you off in that direction?

17

Partnership Potential—Your Choice to Collaborate with Others

Do you believe in partnerships? Do you develop them? If you don't recognize how powerful they are, then do this: Work hard on something for a long time by yourself. When you have maxed yourself out and can do no better, bring in a few qualified people and ask for their help. You will be humbled by how *quickly* they can improve what you were doing, and blessed by how *much* they can improve what you were doing.

If you are not partnering with good people right now, you are not even close to reaching your potential. Ask yourself these questions:

- When was the last time you asked someone to make you better?

- When was the last time you realized someone *could* make you better?
- When was the last time you craved a fresh perspective from others?
- When was the last time you tapped into the thinking of someone else?
- When was the last time you asked for others' advice and opinions?
- When was the last time you got better because someone made you better?
- When was the last time you gave credit to others?

Having partners is like adding one plus one and coming up with three.

To enjoy great partnerships, you need to be a great partner. Recently the John Maxwell Company signed a partnership agreement with the Hendrick Automotive Group. On the official start day, hundreds of leaders from Hendrick joined me and my team to launch this exciting interaction. On behalf of the John Maxwell Company, I spoke to both companies on "The Potential of Partnership." What I shared with them, I now want to share with you.

To be a great partner:

1. Place Their Agenda at the Top of Your Agenda

If you want to partner with others, then be the first to meet them where they are. Find common ground, and place their agenda at the top of your agenda. In essence, become a servant leader, and measure each day by the seeds you sow more than by the harvest you reap.

This step is crucial to a successful partnership. Only when you are on the same page trying to accomplish the same goals is there the kind of synergy that partnerships can provide.

2. Add Value to Them on a Daily Basis

Adding value is the only way a partnership will work. Partnerships begin to disintegrate when one person starts receiving more than they are giving. The only way to be given an opportunity to partner with others tomorrow is to add value to them today. If you want to be a good partner and benefit by increasing your partnership capacity, you need to add value to your partners.

3. Give Them Influence, Ideas, and Tools as Resources

One of my great joys in life is providing resources to people. In the early days when I first began training leaders, I realized that teaching wasn't enough. If I provided people with resources, they were able to go to whole new levels in their leadership. Today, I try to help people by sharing three things with them:

INFLUENCE—WHO DO I KNOW THAT YOU SHOULD KNOW?

Who do you know that your partners should know? How can you connect people who would otherwise never meet? This is a fantastic way to add value to others. It's one of the reasons that every good partnership increases potential relationships.

IDEAS—WHAT DO I KNOW THAT YOU SHOULD KNOW?

How can you help others by sharing ideas? What can you give that they can't provide for themselves? Every time you share an idea, you take nothing away from yourself, but you add tremendously to your partners.

TOOLS—WHAT DO I USE THAT YOU COULD USE?

Tools are systems and practices that are proven to be successful. I have found that systems are the best pathways to achieve desired results. I believe practices are the best behaviors that give desired results. What systems and practices can you share with your partners to help them become better?

4. Tailor Your Service to Meet Their Needs

My first responsibility as a partner is to know you, know your organization, know your needs, and know how I can add value to you. How can I do that? By asking you questions. Questions are the great connectors.

I also work to serve the leaders of my own companies. Every year I ask them, "What can I do to provide a growth environment this year for you?" Each of them has different needs and expectations that I would not know about if I didn't ask. And I try to give them what they need. Leadership by assumption is ineffective.

Are you tailoring what you give according to what your partners need? If you're not, you won't be partners for very long.

5. Never Violate the Trust They Have in You

Trust is the foundation of any solid relationship. Trust can't be established quickly; it must be earned, proven, and tested over time. Once it has been established, your partnerships benefit from a trust advantage, which makes them function more smoothly.

To be a good partner, you need to be dedicated to adding value to others and being faithful to the trust they have put in you.

6. Exceed Their Expectations in Everything You Do

Do you want to develop great partnerships and continue to thrive in them? It's very simple. Consistently exceed the expectations of your partners, and your partnerships will expand. Everyone will want to be a part of whatever you are doing.

7. Respect the Relationship and Grow in It

Too often people gain a partnership and then take it for granted. When that happens, the partnership begins to deteriorate. It becomes strained. And it's only a matter of time before it falls apart. For that reason, I practice gratitude for the partnerships I have, and I also work hard to earn the respect of others. Partnership cannot thrive today on respect that was earned yesterday. It must be continually re-earned.

Do you respect the partnerships you have, whether you earned them yourself or gained them from the work of others? Are you doing the hard work to keep re-earning respect? Don't take for granted the people who work with you or what they bring to the table.

Howard Schultz, the chairman and CEO of Starbucks, said, "Victory is much more meaningful when it comes not just from the efforts of one person, but from the joint achievements of many." I have certainly found that to be true. If you want to take your potential to the highest possible level and achieve more than you ever dreamed possible, then choose to collaborate with others. There's no greater way to increase your potential. And no more enjoyable way.

Partnership Potential Questions

1. Are you naturally a soloist or someone who wants to be part of an ensemble? Do you think of ways to work with others, or do you plan to work alone? How can you change your thinking to develop more partnerships?

2. What work are you currently doing that would benefit from partnership with someone else? Whom could you ask to partner with you today?

3. If you are a leader and have people who report to you, do you think of them as partners you serve or as employees who serve you? How would your capacity increase if you thought of them as partners?

Conclusion

As you finish reading this book, I want you to know that I believe in you, and I believe in your ability to increase your potential. All you have to do is follow this formula:

AWARENESS + ABILITY + CHOICES
= POTENTIAL

If you are aware of yourself and your ability to improve, if you develop the abilities you already possess, and if you make the daily choices that help you improve, you will reach your full potential.

I hope that you now realize that your life need not have limits. As long as you're breathing, you have places to go and ways to grow. You can improve. You can do more. You can make a greater difference. It's all within your reach. My hope and prayer is that you'll seize it.

About the Author

John C. Maxwell is a #1 *New York Times* bestselling author, coach, and speaker who has sold more than twenty-six million books in fifty languages. In 2014 he was identified as the #1 leader in business by the American Management Association and the most influential leadership expert in the world by *Business Insider* and *Inc.* magazine. As the founder of the John Maxwell Company, the John Maxwell Team, EQUIP, and the John Maxwell Leadership Foundation, he has trained more than five million leaders. In 2015, he reached the milestone of having trained leaders from every country of the world. The recipient of the Mother Teresa Prize for Global Peace and Leadership from the Luminary Leadership Network, Dr. Maxwell speaks each year to Fortune 500 companies, presidents of nations, and many of the world's top business leaders. He can be followed on Twitter at @JohnCMaxwell. For more information about him, visit JohnMaxwell.com.

Notes

1. Stephen R. Covey, *Everyday Greatness* (Nashville: Thomas Nelson, 2009), 219.
2. Brian Tracy, "Successful People Are Self Disciplined," Brian Tracy International, http://www.briantracy.com/blog/time-management/successful-people-are-self-discipline-high-value-personal-management/, accessed June 11, 2016.
3. Eph. 3:14–17 (The Message).
4. Eph. 3:17–19 (The Message).
5. John 10:10 (Tree of Life Version).
6. Heb. 8:12 (Living Bible).
7. Eph. 3:20 (The Message).
8. Matt. 9:29 (Berean Study Bible).

Look for John C. Maxwell's other bestselling books

THE POWER OF SIGNIFICANCE

How Purpose Changes Your Life

We all have a longing to be significant, to make a contribution, to be a part of something noble and purposeful. In *The Power of Significance,* John Maxwell gives practical guidance and motivation to get you started on your unique personal path to significance. Learn how to find your why, start small but believe big, seize great opportunities, and live every day as if it matters—because it does!

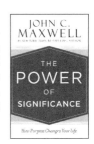

THE POWER OF YOUR LEADERSHIP

Making a Difference with Others

By combining personal passion and leadership, you can discover a whole new level of success. Learn how to attract people to your cause, articulate your vision, and add value to your sweet spot. In *The Power of Your Leadership,* John Maxwell draws on his personal story and provides guidance on how you can become a leader who creates a lasting legacy.

Available now from Center Street wherever books are sold.

Also available in Spanish and from ⌐┘ hachette AUDIO and ⌐┘ hachette DIGITAL

John Maxwell's Bestselling Successful People Series—Over 1.5 Million Copies Sold

WHAT SUCCESSFUL PEOPLE KNOW ABOUT LEADERSHIP

Advice from America's #1 Leadership Authority

The best leaders strive constantly to learn and grow, and every leader faces challenges. Discover actionable advice and solutions as John Maxwell answers the most common leadership questions he receives.

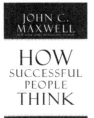

HOW SUCCESSFUL PEOPLE THINK

Change Your Thinking, Change Your Life

Good thinkers are always in demand. They solve problems, never lack ideas, and always have hope for a better future. In this compact read, Maxwell reveals eleven types of successful thinking and how you can maximize each to revolutionize your work and life.

HOW SUCCESSFUL PEOPLE LEAD

Taking Your Influence to the Next Level

True leadership is not generated by your title. In fact, being named to a position is the lowest of the five levels every effective leader achieves. Learn how to be more than a boss people are required to follow and extend your influence beyond your immediate reach for the benefit of others.

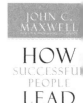

HOW SUCCESSFUL PEOPLE GROW

15 Ways to Get Ahead in Life

John Maxwell explores the principles that are proven to be the most effective catalysts for personal growth. You can learn what it takes to strengthen your self-awareness, broaden your prospects, and motivate others with your positive influence.

HOW SUCCESSFUL PEOPLE WIN

Turn Every Setback into a Step Forward

No one wins at everything. But with this book, John Maxwell will help you identify the invaluable life lessons that can be drawn from disappointing outcomes, so you can turn every loss into a gain.

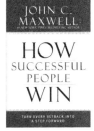

MAKE TODAY COUNT

The Secret of Your Success Is Determined by Your Daily Agenda

How can you know if you're making the most of today so you can have a better tomorrow? By following the twelve daily disciplines Maxwell describes in this book to achieve maximum impact in minimum time.

Available now from Center Street wherever books are sold.

Also available in Spanish and from ⊞ hachette AUDIO and ⊞ hachette DIGITAL

GET IN-THE-MOMENT WISDOM FROM <u>THE</u> LEADERSHIP EXPERT

BREAKAWAY FOR A TAKEAWAY WITH DR. JOHN C. MAXWELL

Sign up today to get the most up-to-date and in-the-moment thoughts from John delivered right to your inbox. As you endeavor toward your biggest dreams and most daunting challenges, don't go it alone.

Receive relevant wisdom and practical insights from John as you

+ Discover your purpose
+ Navigate change
+ Expand your influence
+ Grow daily
+ Live fully
+ Experience lasting significance

PLUS VIP ACCESS TO EVENTS, SPECIAL OFFERS AND EXCLUSIVE UPDATES FROM JOHN!

MINUTE
WITH MAXWELL

Join me each and every day for "A Minute with Maxwell" as I inspire, challenge, and equip you with leadership teachings to apply to your life and career. I am excited to share my short, powerful, FREE video messages with YOU.

Words are vital to communication and leadership. "A Minute with Maxwell" will grow YOUR library of leadership words! Words like *teamwork*, *potential*, *strive*, *connection*, *clarity*—to name a few!

SO WHAT ARE YOU WAITING FOR?
www.JohnMaxwellTeam.com

Mobilizing Christian Leaders to Transform Their World

WHAT ARE WE GOING TO DO FOR PEOPLE WHO MAY NEVER COME TO CHURCH?

FIND OUT MORE HERE | www.iequip.church
678.225.3300